CONTENTS

BODY

MIND

SOUL

DISCLAIMER

This work is solely for personal growth, education, and recreation. It is not a therapeutic activity such as counselling or medical advice and should not be treated as a substitute for any professional advice. In the event of any physical distress, please consult with appropriate professionals. The information and the application of any protocols in this book is the choice of each reader, who assumes full responsibility for his or her understandings, interpretations, and results. The author assumes no responsibility for the actions or choices of any reader.

While all attempts have been made to verify the information provided in this publication, neither the author nor the publisher assumes any responsibility for errors, omissions, or contrary interpretations of the subject matter herein.

No part of this publication may be reproduced, stored in a retrieval system, or transmitted in any form or by any means, electronic, mechanical, photocopying, recording or otherwise, without the written permission of the author. Reviewers may quote brief passages in reviews.

The author of this book does not dispense medical advice or prescribe the use of any technique as a form of treatment for physical, emotional, or medical problems without the advice of a physician, either directly or indirectly. The intent of the author is only to offer information of a general nature to help you in your quest for mental, emotional, and spiritual well-being. In the event you use any information in this book for yourself, the author assumes no responsibility for your actions.

All illustrations, book layout and book cover are created by the author.

FOREWORD

L et me start by saying something very important. Any health advice in this book is about prevention. If you have any pre-existing condition, consult first with your family doctor. Whether you agree with me or not about my way of thinking, teaching or whether you think/believe that what is written in this book is a lie or truth, it doesn't matter. What matters is that whether you believe it or not it has to do with the level of your innerstanding of life. Innerstanding derives from personal experiences.

You have a big pool of thoughts, feelings, and emotions that dictate who you are. If you agree (mostly) with what is written here it means that you resonate with my level. If you don't agree, it does not mean that I am higher or lower than you as everyone is on their own personal journey. If anything written here makes you scoff or if it triggers you, it simply means that there is something in you that needs healing, and then innerstanding. I am the mirror reflecting you, just as you are the mirror reflecting me, indirectly or directly. The more open minded you are, the more bricks you lay in the building of your castle.

The castle can be completed, left halfway built or destroyed, and that depends on the curiosity and yearning for truth that you may have. I will repeat again that whether the content of this book is true or not, it is still a layer of bricks that you build toward your path. How so? By just simply reading someone else's point of view is a lesson for you of how or how not to do something. You will be the judge of it. Health is such an easy way to obtain, and yet most of us take it for granted. Why? Because we are prisoners of conditioning and prisoners of emotions.

There is no scientific or technical language in this book. It's a simple to read book which means it is easier to absorb information and it will not remind you of being in school (indoctrination facility) as you will learn what you want/desire and not what others (teachers at indoctrination facilities/schools) want you to learn. You will see that instead of using the word understand, I will be constantly using the word innerstand. The word understand means standing under someone else's authority while innerstand means to understand from within. Because you are your own authority. You are your own supreme authority, and you are in total charge of your own life. This authority, this sovereignty was given to you by God, your true creator. And nobody else can take this supreme right away from you unless you yourself give it away, whether directly or indirectly.

Readers of my previous book "**I AM THE KEY THAT OPENS ALL DOORS**," are familiar with the term innerstand that I used throughout the book. The more you use this term, the more you go deep within the nucleus of your castle/kingdom. This book is all about personal individual health and it should make you realize how important you are.

HOW CAN YOU HELP CREATING A BETTER WORLD?
Buy local, buy pesticide free produce and products. Ditch animal products as 30-40% of monoculture crops grown are fed on livestock. Healing requires a Holistic approach which focuses on the MIND, BODY and SOUL. They are inextricably linked. Break the conditioning, break the rules (man-made ones).
 Even if you know some or all the words from the glossary page, I suggest you read the description on the meaning of the words as I also elaborated a bit on most of them. Hope you enjoy reading and are a determined person to make the effort to become healthy physically, mentally, emotionally, and spiritually by realizing that you possess the magic pills. Liquids or otherwise.

In this or my other books I use words such as: Maybe, perhaps, possibly, allegedly, it is a fact, an absolute truth and similar words or phrases. It is a personal opinion or fact. You, as a reader treat this or any other book like you would any fictional book so that you do not fall in the trap of satisfying personal beliefs and expectations where you'll end up rejecting information that would eventually prove to be detrimental to you, as opposed to keeping an open mind, which would reward you. When you have no expectations, then you are guaranteed to learn a thing or two from every single book in existence.

English is not the author's mother language.
The message is clear in this book.

DEDICATION

Dedicated to God/Universe/Nature and
all the fragments of it which are YOU,
humans, the multidimensional
immortal heavenly beings

BODY
MIND
SOUL

AS YOU BELIEVE, SO SHALL IT BE

SAIMIR   KERCANAJ

PART ONE

BODY

Feed it life
not death

OTHER BOOKS BY THIS AUTHOR

I AM THE KEY THAT OPENS ALL DOORS
https://www.amazon.com/dp/B095QLZYKM

SELF EMPOWERMENT: BOOK 1
https://www.amazon.com/dp/B09RV37HLC

LIMITLESS POTENTIAL: JOURNEY TO SELF REALIZATION
https://www.amazon.com/dp/B09YV2FSD9

BECOME FREE THROUGH INSIGHTFUL POETRY
https://www.amazon.com/dp/B0B1CXR8C1

GAIN WISDOM THROUGH PRACTICED KNOWLEDGE

YOU ARE NOT A STRAWMAN YOU ARE THE ZYGOTE

breathe

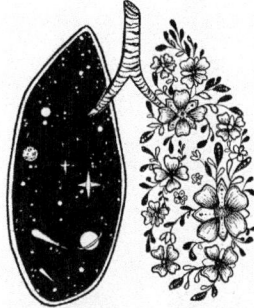

D E E P

Between inhaling and exhaling
*there is the little **DEATH***
The 1st step to a radiant life
*is the way you utilize your **BREATH***

*The food you eat dictates your **HEALTH***
Are you choosing Life?
*or are you choosing **DEATH**?*

*Who is in charge, your belly or your **MIND**?*
If you eat for pleasure and not to be healed,
*Only misery, you will **FIND***
*When you have a healthy body, mind, and **SOUL***
*Only then you will be **WHOLE**.*

S.K.

Chapter ONE

BREATHING IS THE MAIN
NATURAL REMEDY

Disease runs in families because bad habits run in families. To be healthy is to be a rebel. It is the ultimate rebellion in a diseased, sick, dysfunctional society. Most people would think that to be healthy it is important to eat healthy. There is more to health than just what you eat. Being healthy is when you take care of your physical, mental, emotional, and spiritual body. You can go to the gym, drink water, take vitamins all you want but if your head and heart are disturbed with muddy thoughts, you will still be unhealthy.

You are much more than just your physical body. In this first part we will focus on physical health. Breathing is the most underrated health necessity. Humans take it for granted. I am talking about deep breathing and not shallow irregular one where most humans are accustomed to. There are two types of breathing:

Cleansing (exhalation)
Energizing (inhalation)

Energizing breath collects and stores vital energy and focuses more on inhalation. Cleansing breath detoxifies the body and stresses exhalation. The act of breathing not only extracts Chee from air, but it also drives and distributes Chee through the body's invisible network of energy channels, called meridians.

In Asia breathing is regarded as a science. China has its Chee-gung, India has pranayama. The western world lacks a specific term for breath control. Western physicians fail to innerstand how atmospheric energy serves as a vital nutrient for human health. The essential element in air that carries the vital charge of Chee (life-force energy), is neither oxygen nor nitrogen but rather the negative ion, a tiny, highly active molecular fragment that carries a negative electrical charge equivalent to that of one electron.

In nature air is naturally ionized by the action of shortwave electromagnetic radiation from the sun and by the other cosmic rays, which bombard air molecules and impart vital energy to the fragments. Breathing therapy is an established homeopathic medical procedure in Chinese tradition.

And the western world slowly but surely is picking up on it. Deep breathing massages internal organs and glands, purges tissues of toxins, purifies the bloodstream, stimulates hormone secretions, and enhances resistance and immunity. Dr. Sun Ssu-mo wrote about therapeutic deep breathing in Precious Recipes:

When correct breathing is practiced, the myriad ailments will not occur. When breathing is depressed or strained, all sorts of diseases will arise. Those who wish to nurture their lives must first learn the correct methods of controlling breath and balancing energy. These breathing methods can cure all ailments great and small.

Majority of humans take short and shallow breaths into the upper chest area. They receive a small amount of their lung's air capacity. Unfortunately, short, and shallow breaths also stimulate the sympathetic nervous system, the fight or flight response to stress. Because of this, cortisol the stress hormone is released into the bloodstream. This taxes our adrenal glands, and it negatively impacts the whole body.

If this is your unconscious/automatic breathing, then you need to retrain yourself to naturally breathe in a deep and relaxed way. To breathe is to live, to not breathe is to die. Do you know there is a quick pause between breaths? You can think of that as little death. To not breathe is to die, in this case it is about not breathing deeply. Your body is designed to breathe deeply with the diaphragm. Not using the diaphragm means that your body is not functioning the way it is supposed to.

Try to drive the car without having changed the oil when it is required to or if you drive the car as soon as you turn it on without waiting for it to first warm up.

What do you think will happen? At the beginning you might not see a difference but if you continue doing this then the car will start to break down. Now, do you see what can happen if you don't feed the body with prana/Chee (life force energy) the way it is supposed to? It will break down. We could live hundreds of years if we breathed properly, ate properly, think properly, behaved, and felt properly. Every single breath not taken correctly damages you. The damage is accumulative.

The breathing is automatic, and most people take it for granted. You brush your teeth, you walk, you run, you drive a car, or you create art (the process of it, not the actual creativity that requires thinking) or many other things you do in your life. When you learn something of doing it without thinking, that is an automatic habit. Also, your deep breathing has to be automatic.

The way you breathe, controls your life, your look, your energy, your emotions and your resistance to diseases. It controls your very life span.

Wasting semen also controls your lifespan (In PART FOUR there is a whole chapter about how not to and why not to waste semen. If you are a female, you must also read that chapter because it's also about you.). Out of any healthy things you should do, breathing is the most important thing for your health.

You can survive for weeks without food, without water for a few days but you cannot exist for more than a few minutes without breathing. The nutrition provided by air through breathing is more vital to health and longevity than that of food and water through digestion.

"Breath is the spirit of life, the concentrated power or essence of physical being" -Andrew Weil

Aging comes from slowly being asphyxiated from the fact that we have been taught how to breathe backwards from "birth", depriving our Avatar from reaching its full potential. You are an Avatar. Have you watched the movie "**Avatar**?" We are those Blue people. The humans in that movie are the ones that don't want us reaching our full potential. Although externally we are flesh and bones, we are indeed multidimensional avatars.

Breathing improperly is the main problem that we age. 2nd problem (which is important to know) is the belief that we age. The chasing of an unknown future. Competing for more. Celebrating our birthdays and much more that I elaborated in my 1st book "I AM THE KEY THAT OPENS ALL DOORS"

THE CORRECT WAY OF BREATHING

Put one hand on your belly and the other on your chest. The diaphragm is located between your belly and the chest. If you want to know exactly where it is located, put one hand in front of your mouth, a few cm/inches away from it. While the other hand is placed on your belly. Now, pretend that the hand that is in front of your mouth is a candle and try to push the breath out as if you were trying to blow out a candle. When you do that, you will feel a contraction between your belly and your chest,that's where the diaphragm is.

Okay, since now you know the exact location of the diaphragm, keep the hand where you felt the diaphragm and the other on your chest. First inhale deep with your diaphragm until your belly swells/becomes bigger where you cannot put any more oxygen in your lungs, but don't exhale yet. Continue breathing with your chest until you cannot breathe anymore and then exhale slowly until lungs empty completely.

So, by performing a full inhale and exhale you are performing a full breathing (and exhaling) cycle. Filling up both the diaphragm and chest with oxygen is the correct full breathing that you should perform constantly. At first you might forget to do this on a regular basis, so to remind yourself write a few little notes and stick them on your fridge, room door, car's dashboard, on your phone etc.

"Anything you think that is away from the moment, it will turn you into a prisoner of memories (past) and imagination (future)."

Be in the moment my friend, and to achieve that, you should practice **DEEP CONSCIOUS BREATHING** as explained previously. It is not difficult at all to perform it as you were born with that basic ability, you just forgot it in the early years of your life.

Another way of breathing consciously is to focus on the exhale and allow for the inhale. By doing this you are mimicking the natural cycle which is:

Effort to **GIVE**
Relax to **RECEIVE**

Serve and deserve. The act of exhaling is enabling the receiving. The sympathetic nervous system when it governs your life is all about , I want, I need. If you attach this to an economic system, it destroys the world. It is driven by greed, selfishness. The reason for it being destructive is because it never activates the sensation of having received. Besides practicing this Exhale focusing practice, you must also practice *gratitude*. Be grateful for having everything, even if you don't have certain things. You just be grateful and watch how life will change in the long run.

This teaching alone is a big secret to balance. Practice this and you will see a big difference/balance in your life. You will also influence many others as a result of this. Use this as a catalyst for presence and alignment. Surrender not only to the inhale, but also to the exhale for a total detachment (if practiced both techniques- INHALE focusing and/or EXHALE focusing). By focusing on the exhale, then you will naturally inhale what you need in the best way possible. We all must learn how to breathe properly.

CHAPTER TWO

DEEP BREATHING IS YOUR EGO'S ENEMY

"You will become a LIGHT shining on other people's darkness. Your glowing Light will target the direction for those that decide to walk the path. The path to freedom, peace, and immortality."

Deep breathing is your Ego's enemy, while shallow, irregular breathing is your Ego's best friend. What causes shallow breathing? There are many things, but one major thing is not being in the moment. Most of us are carried away by memories of the past or worries of an uncertain future. Any time your mind wanders off away from NOW, you start having shallow, irregular breaths. Many people, if not most, are afraid deep within, from this lifetime and from previous lifetimes.

If you don't believe in reincarnation, then you must not have a purpose for living.

What is your purpose?
I'm sure everyone has had to ask this question. But if you never asked yourself, (consciously of course, unconsciously you already know your purpose, you had to sign an energetic contract before being born) then now definitely is the time to ask this big question. Have you ever analyzed your physical body how it functions? Your feelings, muscles, your eyes, your hearing and other senses, your nervous system, your way of thinking, how you move physically (walking, running, jumping etc).

You are a walking miracle. Do you think you are just born by accident just to go to school (indoctrination facility), work, get married, pay your bills, and die? Think again. These fake reasons to think why we are born only feed destruction of life. We all fell for it. Just like our parents, their parents and so on.

Ego and ignorance breed darkness. You either see darkness as death or as an opportunity to grow. What seems like darkness time, is the womb space between the old and the new. Is like being in the birthing canal. The baby in the womb won't stay there forever, just like you shouldn't linger in the darkness forever but instead use it as an opportunity to grow and innerstand how amazingly of a creation you are.

The simple fact of how you can be alive by breathing is a big feat in itself. The moment you realize and learn how to practice deep breathing, is the moment you plant the seed of creation instead of destruction. If you didn't come from a healthy family, make sure that a healthy family comes from you. Heal what was caused by the past. Heal yourself before trying to heal someone else. When you heal yourself, you heal those around you.

"You will become a LIGHT shining on other people's darkness. Your glowing Light will target the direction for those that decide to walk the path. The path to freedom, peace and immortality."

The 1st step of healing your body, mind and soul is DEEP BREATHING. It's how you starve Ego, by deep breathing. Shallow breathing will eventually cause anxiety, lung problems, weaken the heart, suffering, arthritis, bloating and many, many other conditions. (Remember the car example?). It is of paramount importance that you practice the exercises that are laid out in PART 4 of this book.

Full complete deep breathing can be achieved by filling up with oxygen both your belly and chest. First breathe with your diaphragm (*belly*) until it is full of air then keep breathing with your chest until you can't breathe anymore, release slowly from your nose until all air leaves the lungs, and repeat. This is the correct breathing that should be practiced as many times a day as you can so it can become a habit.

Chapter THREE

DEEP BREATHING PEOPLE
ARE GREAT ACHIEVERS

Your body can achieve high vibrational energy levels but only a few achieve this because they are willing, determined people and make it their mission to generate, utilize and replenish the full capacity of their body/mind energy. High vibration/frequency people are doers and achievers. They have immense vitality and stamina; they are very creative and very athletic and full of energy. Rhythmic breathing is necessary to bring more oxygen into the lungs and bloodstream.

Now, breathe until your lungs are full, hold the breath for 3-4 seconds and exhale slowly. Exhaling must take double the time of inhaling so that there is a balance of the heart rate and evenly oxygenated blood and organs. Perform the above simple but crucial breathing exercise 4-5 times (4-5 inhale/exhales) then continue reading.

Deep breathing benefits:
Breathing is the main food to take in oxygen that fuels your mind and your body. You will function better the more fuel you have. Breathing the right way and effectively, you also live effectively since oxygen powers your thought, your mechanical body. If your mind is clear and healthy, so will your emotions/feelings be. Your life-force energy in the body will be stronger and calmer. Isn't that beautiful? Who would have thought something as simple as breathing can be so powerful and healthy for your wellbeing? God of course, who/what else?

The benefits of effective breathing include:
Increased oxygen intake, relief Of stress, balance of the emotions, relaxation of the body, increased energetic levels, calming of the mind, oxygenation of

the blood, tissues, organs, and muscles. It makes you smarter by oxygenating the front lobe.

SHALLOW BREATHING CAUSES PREMATURE AGING

"The only way to control the future, therefore longevity, is by recognizing the past, learning from it, letting it go and focusing on the present. By performing effectively, the letting go of the past and living in the moment, you have successfully created your future" -S.K.

Very few people are deep breathers. The very fast paced lifestyle, especially in the big, polluted cities is very detrimental for the health of many millions of people around the world. Those people are half alive, by merely functioning. They exist at a low rate of physical and mental vibration. Look around you at people of all ages that are shallow chest breathers except for children. Children are healthier because they have not entered yet the stage of adult stress.

When you have stress and anxiety, you breathe with your chest. This is an unfortunate fact. Try and catch yourself having short breaths when in panic, stress or when anxious for whatever reason. If you breathe deep with your diaphragm, then there wouldn't be a reason to breathe only with your chest. Besides the immediate stress from the everyday fast paced life to survive, stress and anxiety also comes from trying to control what has passed and what hasn't arrived yet. You don't have control over the past or the future (by being anxious).

A little important thing is to not keep in your room the basket with your dirty laundry. You don't want to breathe all night the germs and bacteria. Depending on how many days the dirty clothes are in the basket, they may form fungi/mould and that goes into your lungs. A big part of disease and unhealthy life is internal, either mental or within the house where people are surrounded by chemicals such as deodorants, bathroom air spray, detergents, keeping dirty laundry in the room all night as I mentioned above and something else which is very important is energy stagnancy.

What do I mean by energy stagnancy? In general, we keep furniture and other objects in the house at the same spot. And that is unhealthy. First of all, the way all people's houses are shaped is totally wrong. We are supposed to live in round houses, free of corners. It's what other very advanced loving civilizations lived/live in. A round house, especially with a dome ceiling is the best way to live. First it cannot be destroyed by strong winds as the wind will just curve along the surface, the house will last a lot longer.

And secondly in a round house, with round walls and round ceiling, the energy is never stagnant, the energy will constantly flow and there won't be any space for the low vibrational energies/entities to lurk within the house. An entity doesn't have to be a physical human. It can be immaterial.

Because you cannot see something it does not mean that it doesn't exist. **Did you ever feel the presence of someone that was not there?** Or when you thought that you saw something or someone for a brief second and then you passed it as just an imagination. Yes, that was an entity from a different dimension or the soul/ entity of someone that you know or don't know that exists in this dimension. The entity could be good or bad. To know whether it is good or bad, you got to use your intuition/gut feeling. But if you don't practice deep breathing, if you don't eat healthy, if you don't think healthy your gut/mind/heart will be confused which means you will be confused and will not be able to discern. To end this round house subject because I kind of got carried away, I will strongly suggest that once in a while change the position of the furniture.

Move around pretty much all objects in the house. Including the drawers with clothes where energy is definitely stagnant. By moving around furniture and clothes etc you are moving the stagnant energy, new clean energy will replace the old. Since your house is square, like a box, moving around must be done frequently.

> "The only way to control the future, therefore longevity, is by recognizing the past, learning from it, letting it go and focusing on the present. Performing effectively the letting go of the past and living in the moment, you have successfully created your future."

Deep breathing is very important in general but crucial in awakening and raising the **KUNDALINI**. In the book YOU ARE THE ONE by Pine G. Land, the author has written a couple of useful breathing techniques. Deep diaphragmatic breathing must be a daily routine especially in the days (*check out the book I just mentioned*) when the Moon is in your Sun/zodiac sign. Those are the days when the energy of the Moon and the energy in you is more potent.
It has to do with the planetary alignment at at the time of your birth. Whichever zodiac sign you are, that book has you covered.

Chapter FOUR

FOOD QUALITY EQUALS
LIFE OR DEATH

I t is of paramount importance that you know and innerstand what to eat. The most important aspect of food is how it affects the PH (Power of Hydrogen) of the body. Foods are divided in two categories: Foods that have an acidic reaction in your body and foods that have an alkaline reaction. It is not necessarily related to the PH of the food itself. Alkaline foods are great detoxifiers, they will detoxify the body. The more alkaline a food is, the greater the detoxification that will happen in your body. Fruit is one of the best alkaline detoxifiers.

Alkaline food is your body's best friend. Acidic foods slow, inhibit and stop the detoxification process. Acid-forming foods are inflammatory and mucus-forming, ultimately causing organ failure. Acids can become free radicals causing tissue damage unless linked to an antioxidant (alkaline) and removed. So, if you consume mostly acidic foods, the few alkaline foods that you consume will not be able to remove all the free radicals as the acids are in a much greater number. Disease is a chemical imbalance, simple as that.

The moment the body goes below alkaline levels specifically below the 7HP, it's when disease begins. Food such as fruit and vegetables are chemicals, but good natural ones that are meant to be processed by your body and not lab created poison that is rampant everywhere you go. What you breathe and what you eat affects and regulates the whole body.

The five major organs are super important that they remain healthy. Many people are walking toward their grave and they don't even know it. Their organs are rotten, even if at first glance they don't show it.

The body fights with all it has to keep the five organs operationally at least so they can function at minimum. Eventually the body gives up and disease/death begins the final stage. Technically the person gives up, not the body. The body has already let the person know about the problem throughout life by giving many hints to the person. The five major organs are the five captains.

THE FIVE CAPTAINS

Heart

The heart is called the chief of the vital organs. Your heart regulates other organs by controlling circulation of the river of life or "blood." Your heart houses the spirit. It governs moods and mental clarity. The condition of the heart's health is shown by the colour of the face and tongue. When the colour is dark red, it indicates excess, when it's pale grey it indicates deficiency. The heart is paired with the small intestine, which separates the pure from the impure by-products of digestion, controls the ratio of liquids to solid wastes, and absorbs nutrients, which it then sends to the heart for circulation throughout the body.

Liver

The liver stores and enriches blood and regulates the amount released into the bloodstream for general circulation. When humans move, blood moves when a human is still, blood returns to the liver. This statement accords precisely with the established medical fact that during periods of rest, especially in cold weather, 30-50% of the body's blood supply collects in the liver and pancreas. During sleep, blood is fortified in the liver for use by the rest of the body during activity. The liver houses the human soul (Hun), as reflected in the Chinese term hsin-gan (heart and liver), which means sweetheart or dear. The heart and liver house the most distinctly human attributes. The liver is the body's metabolic headquarters, and it is directly responsible for a person's overall health and vitality. Liver conditions are reflected in the eyes, fingernails, toenails, and muscles. The liver's partner is the gallbladder, whose intimate functional relationship with the liver is well recognized by western medicine.

Pancreas

The pancreas controls production of vital enzymes needed for digestion and metabolism. This function links it directly with its paired Yang partner, the stomach. If the pancreas fails to produce sufficient enzymes, digestion in the stomach stagnates, causing food to ferment and putrefy instead of digest. The pancreas controls the human attribute of rational thought. Its dysfunction is reflected by emaciation of the skin, flesh, limbs, poor muscle tone, chronic fatigue, stagnant digestion, and inability to concentrate.

Kidneys

The kidneys control water. Excess water and fluids are sent to the kidneys and converted into urine, then are passed down to the bladder for excretion. Thus, the bladder is functionally linked to the kidneys as their hollow Yang partner. The kidneys are the gate of life because they control the overall balance of vital fluids in the body, which in turn directly influences energy level and balance. The kidneys are the major balancers of Yin and Yang in the human body.

They house the human attribute of willpower and control the marrow, loins, and lumbar, and sacral regions. Their dysfunction is often indicated by lower back- pains and the inability to straighten the spine. They are closely connected with the adrenal cortex (suprarenal glands), which straddles them and secretes cortisone, adrenaline, and vital sex hormones into the blood stream. The kidneys and their related glands thus control sexual functions and potency.

Lungs
Lungs control Chee/life force energy, state Chinese medical texts. Since Chee means "breath" as well as "energy," the lungs govern both breathing and energy circulation. When breath is deficient, so is energy. The Yin lungs are associated with the Yang large intestine. Lung conditions are reflected in the skin, a fact well known to Western medicine, for the skin itself is a respiratory organ.

Both the lungs and the large intestine are actually internal extensions of the skin., one pushed down from the top, and the other up from the bottom. Pneumonia and other severe respiratory ailments are generally accompanied by constipation, and constipation usually causes distension and discomfort in the chest.

STRESS weakens your heart and brain
FEAR weakens your kidneys
GRIEF weakens your lungs
ANGER Weakens your liver
WORRY Weakens your stomach

HEALTHY GUT
If you want better energy levels, focus, weight, skin, and digestion - it all starts with healthy gut bacteria. 95% of your serotonin, a hormone that influences your mood, is made in the gut. 70% of your immune system is located in the gut. Over 90% of all illnesses are linked to an unhealthy gut. And to have a healthy gut, you must stop consuming dangerous, devoid of life foods. Four of the most harmful foods/chemicals are:

Number 1-**Yogurt**
Not only that yogurt is made with pasteurized milk, which is very dangerous to health, especially causing infertility. Yogurt has added sugar. Sugar is a refined neurotoxin. Sugar is one of the legal dangerous drugs. Beware of

yogurts claiming to give you probiotic benefits. When yogurt is pasteurized, it kills off many of those good bacteria which are very important for a healthy gut. Unless you are making the yogurt home with whole milk (not pasteurized), you won't get enough of the good bacteria benefits to make a noticeable difference in your digestive tract. In 2013 General Mills paid $8.5 million to settle a class action lawsuit that claimed their Greek yogurt was not even a yogurt at all. Also stay clear of any yogurt containing the number one fat forming ingredient high fructose corn syrup.

Number 2- **Wheat bread**

You might have heard that brown bread is better for you than white bread, which can be true, but I say that brown bread is not better than white bread but less harmful than white bread. Saying that brown bread is better implies that the white bread is good, but the brown is better. It's a negative way to condition the mind to accept better one product over the other.

But if you say that brown bread is less harmful than the white, it means that they are both bad. It's that one is worse. Just by changing this way of thinking, you can make a big improvement in your life. This was just an example about bread, but it applies to other foods or areas in life. Back to wheat. Many big companies are taking advantage of you. Wonder Bread Stone Ground 100% Whole Wheat contains large amounts of the number one fat forming ingredient high fructose corn syrup. A 2004 study done at the University of Louisiana Medical Centre by Dr. George A. Bray, linked high fructose corn syrup to the siding rate of obesity. Why is high fructose corn syrup so bad?

It is 20 times sweeter than sugar. Fructose is a chemical that isn't recognized by our brain. It confuses your ghrelin, which is the hormone that tells you when you are hungry. It also disrupts leptin production, which is the hormone that tells you that you are full. When these two hormones are out of balance, you never know when you're full. SO, what does your body do?

It tells you to eat more and more. Dr. David Kessler, former head of the Food and Drug Administration even appeared on CBS News, exposing how high fructose corn syrup literally forces your brain to make you eat more than you should. I'm surprised the News channel or should I say FAKE NEWS would allow it to air.

One thing our bodies are extremely good at is turning unknown substances into fat. The reason we do this, dates to how our bodies were designed many thousands of years ago when we got our food by hunting and gathering. Because we never knew when the next meal was coming. Our bodies would store fat in case of tough times. When you consume things like high fructose corn syrup or sugar, things our bodies were never designed to digest, our bodies get confused. The body does the only thing it knows how to do with foreign substances, it adds it to your waistline, love handles or butt.

BEWARE of any food that contains high fructose corn syrup. You might as well be pouring fat into your waistline. It is very important that you innerstand how the chemicals are harmful to your health and how the body reacts.

When you have an innerstanding, you become the captain of the ship (body). I, personally, have been on a healthy lifestyle for 7 or so years. I knew that high fructose syrup was harmful, but I still consumed once in a while food that contained this dangerous chemical. I continued because I didn't innerstand of the destruction process that was taking place in my body.

When I innerstood how the body reacts to this death chemical, then I stopped consuming it for good. These few examples are just a sample, but there are thousands of harmful chemicals in everyday foods that people consume without a second thought. It's very simple to see if a food is healthy or not.

Just check the ingredients- most foods have ingredients that are difficult to spell and also a deceiving wording is used. For example, the word "spices." As a customer, you read it and think "Oh, it's just spices," but that is actually a chemical cocktail. A product that has a long list of ingredients is not food but junk. Healthy food doesn't need to be advertised. Anything that has an ad, must not be consumed.

So, instead of you going crazy by checking every time all kinds of packaged foods, which you will never win by the way since you don't even know if they are being truthful. If they actually put a list of dangerous chemicals, rest assured that the list is much longer, it's just not printed at the back of the package. Here is another scam/deception by the poison industry, oops I meant food industry.

The hydrogenated oil

Hydrogenated oil comes in two forms: partially or fully hydrogenated. One use of hydrogenated oil is to preserve the shelf life of food. Partially hydrogenated oil contains trans fats that can raise cholesterol and result in health complications. In 2015 Food (Chemical/poison) and Drug Administration FDA said that partially hydrogenated oil is not safe and removing it from food could prevent thousands of heart attacks each year. I can say two things about this topic regarding FDA:

1- Why was it legal in the first place before they decided to withdraw it. Was there an experiment on the guinea pigs (humans) first and see how far they could go before withdrawing it from the marker. Assuming it was withdrawn.

2- For the FDA to make that decision it means that the hydrogenated oil (artificial one) was very bad. And by law if a product has less than 0.5 of hydrogenated oil/trans fats the companies are not required to label it or print it on the package. Now, you tell me, is it ok? Is it moral? Whether it is 10% or 0.1% it should not be consumed by humans at all, period. And who makes the law? Who pays those that make the law?

Corporations of course, so the law will be made to satisfy the requests of those that have to gain in selling their own products, don't you think? You are responsible for your health, don't expect those that gain from your sickness to care about you. To be healthy first you must let go of what made you unhealthy in the first place. As the father of medicine Hippocrates said:

"If someone wishes for good health, one must first ask oneself if he is ready to do away with the reasons for his illness. Only then is it possible to help him"

Number 3 - **Cereal bars**
Kellogg's Special K is marketed as one of the premier healthy cereals on the shelf, and yet in Special K Red Berries Chewy Snack Bar, sugar is a component of the second ingredient and then emerges again as corn syrup. Oats and chocolate bars contain corn syrup, sugar, sugar cane fiber, and fructose (or death). Honey Nut Cheerios' milk and cereal bars have sugar, brown sugar syrup, corn syrup, high fructose corn syrup and plain fructose. So, the above is a recipe for weight gain and death.

Number 4 - **Fat-free Deception**
There is one fat substitute that you must never consume, no matter what. This poison fat free food is marketed to you as a healthy food which is not food at all but **dig a 6 feet hole in the ground** food. Fat-free potato chips is the supposed health food I'm talking about. The scientific invention behind this fat-free snack is Olestra. Olestra was created by Procter and Gamble (I guess gambling with people's lives) to be a calorie and cholesterol free fat substitute. You might know it as Olean.

But the name may have changed. When more and more people figure out companies' deception, they change names, just like aspartame, another super dangerous lab made chemical that has been marketed under different names for the gullible people. Olean, this fat-free substance is way worse than gluten or other carbs you can eat. This is because it blocks your body from absorbing essential vitamins A, D, E, K. Common reactions include diarrhea, cramps, and leaky bowels. Whatever you do, do not eat this nasty carb. There are more dangerous carbs like Olean out there.

The food conglomerates are inventing new ones all the time. By the time people catch on to it, a lot more uglier poisons have been invented. So, you can never keep up with this so that's why it is wise to only consume fruit, vegetables, nuts, herbs, grains so pretty much all food that is grown on the ground. The food must be eaten in its rawest form with the exception of when you need to cook the vegetables, but even then, you must cook them in low heat, stir fry them. If you overcook the food, you destroy all the enzymes, proteins etc no matter how good the food may taste. Unless you grow the food yourself, it is nearly impossible to know what you are putting into your body. Because of the high fructose syrup and other chemicals disrupting your hunger/being full of hormones, you will always be in trouble unless you put the body in homeostasis where the body regulates itself. But the body will not regulate itself if you prevent it by suffocating your body with chemicals. In PART FOUR of this book, you will see/read the super healthy routine that you can put your body in a homeostasis state. Guaranteed. But you must follow it. You can't be super healthy in just one day. It took years of accumulated poison to make you sick, but it doesn't mean that it will take years to fix it. The signs of reversing your health toward positiveness should show within weeks for some or months for others, depending on how determined you are.

> *I don't believe in cheat days. I believe the cheat days must have been invented by lazy people or people pleasers. Who do you think you are going to cheat, your neighbour? Of course not. You only cheat yourself. The more cheating you do, the closer to the cliff you're approaching.*

This was a very short list out of thousands and thousands of garbage, poisonous food out there that millions of people consume, unfortunately. I could go on and on about what not to eat which could take up most of the book. But it's more efficient to know what to eat and you won't have to focus and waste energy on what not to eat because you cannot keep up with changes/deception from the corrupt mega corporations.

When you learn the short list of what to eat, then no need to worry about the long list of poisons. By all means do your own research. There are a lot of books out there that have done a great job at exposing Big pHARMa and the medical system (mafia). Which I will not go in detail here as the purpose of this book is to provide a healthy routine that you can follow. A book that I suggest is the book that opened my eyes 7 years ago when I realized that we are controlled by tyrants.

The book is called "Natural Cures they don't want you to know about" By Kevin Trudeau. He was great at exposing. If you research this author, you may see articles depicting him as a fraud. Many that fight against tyranny, are depicted as charlatans, frauds etc. Most people when they search on a search engine, they click on articles that are on the first page. In the first page the algorithm decides that you read what THEY want you to read. So, when you research, use more than one search engine and dig deeper.

Anyway, you can check out this book or other books, up to you. I suggest you do not buy the mass market paperback as it's what I got, and it has very small letters. Top notch info by the way. (All mass market paperback books have small letters, difficult to read). It is strongly recommended to consume alkaline foods. Some alkaline superfoods that you should be consuming regularly are:

kale, bananas, mushroom, figs, papaya, olives, squash, okra, hemp onion, spelt, kamut, oranges, dates, apples, melons, bell pepper, berries, cucumber,

Brazil nuts, walnuts, Key limes, cherries, watermelon, Hemp seed, avocado, ginger, mango   , wild rice.

They boost your immune system, increase energy, help fight disease and keep you overall healthy. Not all these foods are available all year round but use whatever is available in the season. Never eat fruit after a regular meal, especially cooked one. First you should consume food that doesn't take a long time to digest such as fruit, and then food that takes hours such as solid cooked food or even nuts, because the fruit will ferment if it's consumed after let's say cooked food or rotten cooked flesh(meat). It takes hours to digest processed foods or cooked meat (which you should not consume anyway).

When you have fruit for example, it will stay on top or mixed with the cooked food. By the time the cooked food has left the stomach, the light food (the ones that doesn't take long to digest such as fruit) will ferment and create disease instead of healing.

HOMEMADE RECIPES

Homemade Toothpaste
3 tbsp Coconut oil, 1tbs aluminum free baking soda (make sure the package says aluminum free, it is very important)- baking soda and mix them until it becomes like a paste. Add more coconut if it's too thick or more baking soda if it's too thin/watery, 3-4drops of hydrogen peroxide 3%.
Right now, I'm using only Coconut oil and baking soda. You can add a couple of drops of mint (or lemon, grapefruit or whichever you prefer) essential oils (food grade).

Raw Apple Cider Vinegar.
Fill a Mason jar ¾ of the way with apples or apple scraps. Stir honey into warm water until dissolved. Pour sweetened water over the apples. Leave 2-3 inches of room at the top of the jar. Cover with cheesecloth, thin fabric or coffee filter and a rubber band or Mason jar screw-top lid. Set in a warm, dark place for two weeks. Place it on a warm surface and cover with a tea towel. After two weeks, strain out the solids, pressing on them gently to extract the extra liquid. At this point it tastes wonderful.

Apple cider vinegar is simply fermented apple cider. Set the fermented cider in a warm, dark place for about four weeks. The apple cider vinegar is complete when it has a strong apple cider vinegar smell and taste. Allow to ferment longer if you think it is not strong enough. If you notice a mother culture forming on top, do not be alarmed. That is normal. Do not throw away that mother culture as that is the most important of the whole thing. When ready to drink the apple cider vinegar, shake the jar well so the mother culture spreads everywhere.

Homemade Hot Chocolate

Making hot chocolate is super easy. Simply put a tablespoon of cocoa in a mug and pour hot water on it. That's it. Make sure it is organic. The organic food will cost more than the non-organic one, but it will last for a long time as you will only use a spoon at a time. Cocoa by itself is not sweet so if you need to sweeten it up, just add some honey or coconut sugar. DO NOT use any white refined sugar for this or for anything else.

Homemade Milk (JUICE)

Here is another easy one to do. First of all, homemade can be called juice and not milk, unless you just had a baby then of course you can have a homemade milk. Just make sure you label it, so your husband/partner doesn't drink it by mistake.

Okay, let's move on how to make homemade juice, or milk if you'd like to call it that. You can make milk out of any nut in the nut family. (don't think dirty). Just put a handful of walnuts or any other kind of nut such as pecans, cashews etc in a mixer. Add water and mix it until it's all grind and voila, you have homemade milk. But you must strain it before you drink it.

Especially almonds as you would not be able to drink it without straining it first. Use a strainer or a cheese cloth or you can buy online a synthetic strainer that you can easily rinse with water and soap. Depending on the desired consistency you decide how much water you put in the mixer. Use the mixer that you make smoothies.

Homemade Peanut Butter

To make peanut butter, you just need peanuts. I suggest you use raw, unsalted ones. You need a coffee grinder. Make sure that the coffee grinder you have or one that you buy says that it also grinds nuts. You need this kind of grinder so it can grind the peanuts into a powdery state.

Peanuts are oily, so maybe a couple of times while grinding them move the amount round while in the container. Grind first the peanuts by themselves until they become like a powder. Then add a few drops of oil, preferably grapeseed oil or avocado oil. You can use olive oil also but olive oil it kind of smells.

I personally love olive oil but for peanut butter it may change a bit the way it tastes and smells, so I use either avocado oil, or grapeseed oil. If you have vegetable oil in the house, throw it in the garbage as all vegetable oils, especially cheap ones, are pure poison. These are just some examples of homemade stuff. There is a lot more that you can do. A simple search on the internet or other books that have lots of recipes there that you can do.

Chapter **FIVE**

DISEASE STARTS FROM WITHIN

Anything external reflects internal and vice versa. Unfortunately, our world has been poisoned everywhere in the form of polluted air, smog, pesticides, herbicides, fake chemical flavours and so on. Just in our homes our walls are loaded with chemicals. Not everyone. Just make sure and research if formaldehyde is used in your house. The buildings in general are built with toxic materials such as formaldehyde, a very toxic substance. Formaldehyde is used to make walls, cabinets, and furniture. Many contractors continue to use this dangerous toxic chemical as a preservative.

Formaldehyde can make you sick if you breathe in too much. Formaldehyde is known to cause CANCER. It can irritate the airways, so people with respiratory problems such as bronchitis, asthma and other breathing conditions are especially sensitive to toxic formaldehyde.

"Ignoring the power of self-healing is the worst crime/sin you can do to your body. One way or another, sooner or later your body will reflect your choices" -S.K.

In the above quote where it says about self-healing, it doesn't mean that you can eat and think whatever you want, and the body will take care of itself. No, no. The body will heal itself but only after you put your body in the right conditions.
Those conditions are:

Deep breathing
Adequate water consumption
Raw fruit/veggie/nuts consumption
Positive thinking
Meditation
Fasting and much more that will
be explored in **PART Four.**

There is a longer list of an amazing proven health routine in **PART FOUR.** Let me tell you about what I mean by PROVEN. Before I tell you, first I must ask you to look around you in this world where we all are part of? What do you see? Sick or healthy people? Mostly sick people even if you don't realize that, let alone that if you read this in the middle of the pLandemic you can clearly see that we are a very sick society where people don't trust oxygen or their immune system.

But let's pretend that you believe there is actually a virus going on so let's skip the **PLAN**demic (had to type in bold, in case you didn't catch the truth when I only used the letter "**L**" before) and go up to the point before this cartoon situation started. How come there are millions and millions of people on medication? And more and more young poor souls are on medication. That should make you puke that we are carrying these amazingly created biological bodies, and at the same time a big chunk of humanity is sick and diseased.

Why do more and more people get sicker and sicker, depressed, anxious, worried? WHY, WHY, WHY? One of the main reasons is that people haven't been taught the healing abilities that they possess. Don't you worry, I will get to the point of what I meant by "PROVEN"

By lacking in obtaining knowledge, people give their power to the powers that be. The medical system (**MAFIA**, yes, capital letters and bolded) profits on people being sick and on medications for life. Since the mafia needs constant revenue, they pay the main health organizations (they all are in bed with each other) so that the people get fed whatever information these CORPorations/ organizations want. The information is lies, deception. There are many articles, books, ads, public figures, tv shows figures that promote-wait wait, ok here is coming - PROVEN remedies, medications and so on and so on. Who approved them?

Were you following the tests of the medications? Were the studies independent? I can go on and on but I'm sure you get what I mean. So, as for the PROVEN health routine in Part 4, it is APPROVED by me and many others like me that think for ourselves and whatever information we give is honest, genuine with the intention to help humanity. By approving the routine in PART FOUR it means I (and others) personally experience the routine, we are not mainstream doctors that have to feed patients what the scums behind the scenes want us to sell.

If you are one that beLIEves that an information is true only when a person in white coat (legal drug dealer) says so, then I got bad news for you. That you are ruled by heartless criminals. But if you are reading this book, wouldn't that mean that you are already suspecting that healthcare is disease care?

This is generalizing the medical system. I'm sure there are many doctors that have good intentions but have been caught in the scheme of those above them. But it is not an excuse, if a doctor develops high consciousness and empathy then he/she would have to leave their job and pursue and become homeopathic. When you know that something is harmful to a human body, you are morally obligated to not give it to another person. Even if that person doesn't know any better but asks for it anyway. Knowledge means responsibility. When you know and innerstand you carry a big responsibility with you.

You cannot close your eyes when they are open to knowledge and innerstanding. Other harmful products that most if not all people have/use at home on a regular basis. Some of those are: Toothpaste with fluoride and other chemicals used for whitening the toothpaste and to become foamy when you brush your teeth. Or bathroom deodorants for bad bathroom smell. When you spray those chemicals in the bathroom after you done with #1, 2 or 3 (3=1+2 together:), the bad smell doesn't go away at all. It's the poisonous chemical that suppresses your smell sensors.

For a temporary inconvenience you receive a poisonous, cancerous chemical. The soap, or conditioner you use for your body, or hair is loaded with chemicals. Unless you have done your homework and bought the best healthy products, or you make them yourself home. Detergent for your hands, dishwasher, laundry is full of chemicals. And these are just a few.

Another very dangerous thing for your health to have at home is the microwave. The microwave kills the life force energy of the food therefore, the food becomes devoid of life no matter how good it smells. Also, the water that you have in the house is loaded with fluoride, chlorine, and other harmful agents. The water is from the sewage. **You thought that the tap water and the one that you shower is from the springs of Fiji?** Invest in a filter, at least shower head filter. Your skin is the biggest organ in your body, it absorbs the contaminated water. So, you see? Just a few items that you regularly use and have at home contribute to the weakening and shortening of your lifespan.

CONDITIONING HAS DISTORTED CRITICAL THINKING

People question healthy diets, they want the source of information or studies done about fruit, veggies, fasting etc, but have no problem ingesting pills, processed food, alcohol, refined sugars/flowers, and other garbage produced by this corrupt heartless devoid of life system. Having consumed devoid of life food, damages your physical, mental, emotional, and spiritual body. When not enough oxygen is not received by the brain, especially the front part that is responsible for logic, a person is dumbed down.

Ask any person you want if they think they are dumbed down, nobody will answer with "yes." And that's because we hear ourselves daily and are familiar with whatever level of logic, we think we are; therefore, we only think others are dumbed down. That's Ego in high gear thinking for us. Medicine is not healthcare. Medicine is sick care. Raw food is healthcare. Food produced by Mother Earth. Any food that does not come from the ground must not be consumed.

The bitter truth is that our society has been going on for a very long time through a conditioning that has made people escape reality. Reality is what you make it out to be. In our society many unfortunate young people and adults are addicted to drugs. Or should I say that they are addicted to escaping reality. Outside reality is a projection of your inner reality. See? You or someone else may detest this world full of famine, wars, greed etc. I don't detest it as I think this world is beautiful.

I know and I am very aware of the condition of our society, but I chose to radiate love and positivity. In the process I have affected many people with my radiance. **You must consciously create your reality and not be reactive to your unconscious thoughts and actions.** When you acknowledge that you create your reality, then opportunities to heal will present themselves as you will be the conductor of the orchestra (thought, emotions, activities, verbal expressions etc)

Chapter **SIX**

BREATHE LIFE INTO EVERY CELL

B reathing is one of the body's strongest self-healing mechanisms. One single automatic thing that you do every second which is breathing, can heal you but only when you breathe properly and fully. Some of the benefits of breathing are:

It lowers blood pressure
Reduces heart rate
Decreases stress hormones
Makes (it purifies it) healthier blood
Enhances physical and mental energy and clarity
Improves immunity

Deep breathing broadens your aura so you can attract everything you desire. Breath is how we meditate, and meditation is how we grow our aura. Aura is how we connect to the Universal energy (innerG). Attracting the universal energy is how we turn thoughts to matter in this reality. Breath is how you turn a thought into a real matter that you can experience on this planet (planET). It is physics proven in our physical labs. In between breaths, death resides.

Not the physical death that humanity thinks of as not existing anymore, which is an illusion by the way. What it actually means is the EGO is dead/ non-existent in between breaths. The Ego needs thoughts to function, so in between breaths (metaphorically) while meditating is when the magic happens.
Meditation is a subject for another chapter which is as crucial as deep breathing. Because breathing is crucial for your physical health, while not breathing (metaphorically speaking again) while deeply meditating where you are unconscious, you meet God which resides within you and outside

of you. You can be at 2 places at once while meditating. The experiment of Michelson and Morley proved it. You can also prove it yourself by innerstanding and practicing the relation between Body-Mind-Soul.

Without oxygen life cannot exist. It is not just oxygen or carbon dioxide but the life force energy that the air carries. Your lungs are food for the trees and vice versa. Half of your lungs are on the trees. You expel carbon dioxide to feed the trees and the plants, while they expel oxygen to feed you. When you innerstand this simple amazing fact, your moral compass should rise exponentially. Get comfortable. Lie on your back in bed or on the floor with a pillow under your head and knees.

Or you can sit in a chair with your shoulders, head and neck supported against the back of the chair. Breathe in through your nose. Let your belly fill with air. Breathe out through your nose. Place one hand on your belly and one hand in front of your mouth and blow the air as if you were to blow out a candle. When you do this, you will feel muscle contraction in your belly and that's where your diaphragm is. It's how you can easily locate your diaphragm. Place one hand on your belly and the other on your chest.

As you breathe in, your belly will rise, as you breathe out your belly will lower. The hand on your belly should move more outwards than the hand on your chest. That means that you are also using your diaphragm to breathe instead of only your chest. Breathing with your chest, you exist, breathing with your diaphragm and the chest, you live, you make the best out of it (body).

Chapter SEVEN

BE YOUR OWN DOCTOR

"The preservation of health is a duty. Few seem conscious that there is such a thing as responsible physical morality" -Herbert Spencer

I f you do not take charge of your body and mind, then you will depend on the doctors. Only you know what's best for you. Doctors test many medicines on people. You know, like when a prescription pill doesn't work then they tell you to try a new one, meanwhile the previous prescription has already done the damage. Doctors are taught to put a patch on the problem instead of looking for the cause of it. If you go to the doctor, it is like not having a mind of your own. If you are someone that will scoff or get triggered at this than ask yourself these questions to yourself:

Who am I?
What Am I?
Do I have the capability to think for myself?
Do I have the capability to heal myself?
How does my body function?
How are my body, mind and soul connected?
Why are there more and more people getting sick?
Why don't the doctors promote healthy eating, exercise, and nutrition before resorting to lab made pills?
Why does the doctor ask what is wrong with me when I go and see him/her for my ailment?
If the doctor asks to know what is wrong with me, then why do I go to seek help when I am the only person possessing the answer?

Every disease has its roots in the way you feed your body. Whether you breathe properly or whether you eat properly. Every disease is simply a chemical imbalance. Every disease is caused by mucus. Mucus is formed by lifeless food. Meaning food of low vibration such as processed food, rotten flesh (meat), alcohol, soft drinks, and many thousands more products that have taken the life out of humanity.

"All diseases begin in the gut"
-Hippocrates

Happy, strong, healthy people who accomplish greatness are those of faith that possess a deep spiritual philosophy. Life is philosophy. Life is a game. We are all players in it. Will you be a main player striving for freedom and greatness or stay on the bench and let life pass away from your grasp?

Chapter EIGHT

SKIN IS THE BIGGEST ORGAN
IN YOUR BODY

E very 35 days or so skin replaces itself, the liver replenishes itself in about a month. Your body creates new cells based on the food you eat. What you eat becomes literally you. If you eat healthy, healthy cells will be created. If you eat unhealthily, then cancerous, oxygen deprived cells will be created. Smoking Besides destroying your lungs and overall health, smoking destroys your skin also. If you are a smoker, your wounds will take longer to heal, plus it worsens skin diseases since the pores of the skin must be free and get oxygenated regularly. Sunscreen. The sunscreen is very bad for your skin and your health.

Unfortunately, throughout the decades humanity has been misled to beLIEve that sunscreen protects you from getting cancer. It is a big lie. Sunscreen gives you cancer. The reason for it is that besides the sunscreen having toxic chemicals as ingredients, but also the sunscreen blocks your skin pores that the sun must go through. The sun equals LIFE. The sun is not your enemy, mucus is. Like the great nutritionist Arnold Ehret said:

"After several months on a mucusless diet with sun baths, we looked like Indians and people believed that we belonged to another race"

Now, there is absolutely nothing wrong with the sun. The problem is how healthy/unhealthy your biological vehicle (body) is. Although you are not supposed to stay for a long period of time under the sun from noon till 4-5pm, you could get cancer if you don't take sun baths regularly. You can't expect your body to become healthy in a very short period of time by sunbathing once in a blue moon.

Your body is loaded with toxins, puss, and other residues from polluted air (if you live in a city) and processed foods etc. So when/if you get cancer, it is because of the reaction of your body from the intense heat of the sun.

The sun is doing its job, but you also have to do yours by keeping your body in the right conditions. We live in a fast-paced environment lifestyle, and most year around we try to gain what is lost by using temporary supposed solutions. Not only that the sunscreen is a band aid that will not resolve anything, but it is a bad, rotten band aid that not only will not make you better, but it will make you worse. If you are lucky enough to live in a village or away from the polluted city you have been blessed and can enjoy the sun at will. As am I. I lived for 30 years in a city environment.

Fortunately, for over 10 years I have been living away from the city lifestyle or should I say disease style. And I have taken advantage of nature and the sun of course. If you sunbathe regularly, you will not get burned or get skin cancer even if you sunbathe between 4-5pm which is the timeframe that the sun is the hottest. If you live in the city do not get discouraged though. All cities have parks. Go to any park and sunbathe. Assuming you live in an apartment that the sun is obstructed. Or go to the beach, lake, river, mountain etc.

There is no excuse. Nature has provided us with anything for us to live healthy. It all depends on us to align with mother nature (GAIA), and she will take care of us. If you have any sunscreens in the house, throw them in the garbage. It doesn't matter how much you paid for it. No price can beat the pricelessness of your health. Another advice I can give is to not shower/bathe every day. Unless you work in a job where you get dirty and sweaty every day. Your skin has millions of pores but also an oily substance to keep your skin moisturized. So, when you bath/shower many times a week you destroy the needed oily substance and problems can arise.

The wastes and toxins of your body are expelled through your lungs (exhaling), feces and your skin. If your skin is clogged or damaged (even if it doesn't look damaged visually it doesn't mean that it's not underneath of it), then those toxins that were supposed to be expelled from it would put more strain on your lungs and also will accumulate under the skin and block the pores.

And when the pores are blocked with toxins, puss etc, guess what happens when the sun hits your skin. That's right, CANCER happens. I'm inclined to repeat that there is nothing wrong with the sun. The sun's rays only react to your actions.
   Action-Reaction. For every action (or inaction) there is an equal reaction. Doing nothing (about something) it's also like doing something. Which means by not doing something about your health, in this case your skin, you cause the creation of cancerous cells. I suggest you moisturize your skin with coconut oil or aloe vera. Aloe vera is antiseptic.

KEY POINTS
Don't bathe every day.
Don't sunbathe between 12-5pm (12:00-17:00).

Don't wear sunglasses as they stop the healthy gamma sun rays which you need for your pineal gland (third eye).
Do not use any sunscreen, no matter how healthy the package claims to be.
Do not look at the sun directly after 9am-6pm.

FEED YOUR BODY JUST LIKE YOU WOULD FEED YOUR PLANTS

Feed your and kids' bodies with oxygen, water, sun, just like you feed the plants and not sodas or sugary poisons. You wouldn't feed your plants with let's say soda (soft drinks) for example, would you? I used this soda example because it reminded me of the movie **IDIOCRACY**, a 2006 movie. I suggest you watch it. Plants/fruit that give us life receive water, sun, and nutrients from the soil. It's what we should consume also.

Anything made in the factory or lab is not food but **DEATH**. Semen ejaculation shortens life. The belief that you get older also contributes to premature aging. I elaborated on why we age in my last book I AM THE KEY THAT OPENS ALL DOORS.
Pineal gland is the master gland regulator. It's a big subject in itself so most likely I will elaborate on my next book

TOP TEN DOCTORS

1 WATER
2 REST
3 MEDITATIONS
4 DEEP DIAPHRAGMATIC BREATHING
5 FASTING
6 SUN
7 BE IN NATURE
8 NATURE
9 EXERCISE
10 RAW FRUIT/VEGGIES

Meditation is praying, giving gratitude to anything you have. Many pray to have things, that's not praying, that's a Satanist mindset.

God gave you everything, it's only a matter of aligning your vibration with the same vibration of those things which is love, gratitude. Your body needs light. The raw food and breathing properly, equals Light, health. Nurture your physical body with raw food, sun, water, air. SIMPLE. The next PART is "The MIND." The mind can destroy the body if your mind is not clear of negative thought. You and only you are responsible to have a fertile or a baren body and MIND, so let's move on to that chattering monkey called "the Mind."

PART TWO

<u>MIND</u>

NOTHINGNESS
IS FULL OF
MAGIC

Solitude

What everyone needs is:
To listen to our inner voice
To be authentic
To be original
To be creative
To get inspiration
To be at peace
To return to ourselves

   -TUYEN

Chapter **ONE**

STUDY YOUR MIND

I t is so sad that we are such a powerful species, designed masterfully, and yet our potential is inhibited by external conditioning. We are conditioned to behave and process life in a constant pattern of self-harm that never allows us to reach our true potential as multidimensional human beings that we are. One such conditioning is "studies." People get influenced by studies.

Especially when it is about health. The mind is constantly bombarded by many supposed studies, but also by genuine honest studies, articles, magazines, advertisements, memes, quotes etc. By listening or reading repeatedly about studies, the mind creates a beLIEf and subsequently the mind does not question the validity of the source of the study because the brain has already registered it as a supposed truth. Always you must have questions.

Was it an independent study or not?
Who is behind the studies?
Are there any personal gains for the purpose of the studies?
Were the studies done for the betterment of society in mind or for personal gain?

You cannot fix your problems; you can only fix your thinking and the problems will fix themselves. **When you change the way, you look at things, the things you look at, change**. The quality of your life depends on the quality of your thinking.

> *You can grow a rose, or you can grow a bush. Both will thrive, the only difference is that one will bring you life and the other will give you death. Would you invest in living or in dying? Would you rather talk to yourself, pretend to talk to yourself or talk to others thinking that you are talking to yourself?*

SOLITUDE is THE ANSWER,
A sovereign man/woman cannot be CONtrolled/governed. Your beliefs should be subjected to change, as you acquire and analyze new information daily. If you don't agree, then you're not seeking the truth. You're seeking validation. And by seeking validation, you dig deeper into the hole of your burial. Resign from the distorted Matrix prison. Free your mind. Unlearn everything that you have been culturally conditioned to and relearn from scratch, just like a baby that is untainted.

"We are caged by our cultural programming.
Culture is a mass hallucination, and when you step outside the mass hallucination you see it for what it it's worth"
-Terence McKenna

He who stands on tiptoe
doesn't stand firm.
LET IT GO
He who rushes ahead
doesn't go far.
He who tries to shine
dims his own light.
He who defines himself can't know who he really is.
He who has power over others
can't empower himself.
He who clings to his work
will create nothing that endures.

If you want to accord with the Tao,
just do your job, then let go.

Lao Tzu
Tao Te Ching

Chapter **TWO**

HOW TO UNMANIPULATE YOURSELF

I n the grand scheme of things, we were/are all ignorant. If this upsets/ triggers you, then you need internal healing. Even if you believe it to be a true statement, you still have a long ways to go. A person that thinks is intelligent, will never progress fast, he will only progress slowly to a certain degree by observing others. That kind of progress is superficial. To progress at a faster rate, you must have personal experiences. You must experience new things every day, instead of following a mundane routine. Most people remain ignorant for many reasons, but two major ones according to my personal life experience are:

1- Refusing to open their mind

Know that everyone is your teacher. You are also my teacher because by authoring this book for you the whole universe moved so I could do research, think deeply, recalling all my life experiences, observing others, and be in contact with many people that I know personally or people I only know from social media. All these actions done to write this book, it also expanded my mind, my consciousness. Every person you meet is your teacher regardless of if you look down on someone or not.

If you do look down on someone for being of a lower level than you, then you are already lower than that person.

Be humble and pay attention to everything that is being said to you and if you have to deal with people that are mean, that make fun of you or anything that they might say to you, just observe their behavior without being invested emotionally, record in your mind their behavior. Other people's behavior is your teacher. Keep a journal, a notebook of things people say or do even if those things they say may not seem important to you now. One day those things can be very useful to you.

"You can fit in your mind as much information as you allow yourself to"
Subconsciously you will learn many things. Those things can be good or bad depending on if you are conscious regularly about what you eat, hear, say etc. You can learn from two different ways, one from others and from yourself. If you function subconsciously, meaning whatever you do and say every day you do those things as a habit, without being aware and analyzing them, then those things (whatever is that you do or say) are not your teacher, they are your enemies that can bury you because anything you say or do will have a reaction from the outside world.

You will accumulate bad or good karma depending on if you live your life by being conscious and aware of why you do the things you do or by habit which by the snowball effect you will harm yourself and those affected by your choices. You will innerstand about how you get punished or rewarded by your actions on the UNIVERSAL LAWS section. Be grateful for learning from others even if they are unaware. If you are grateful, rest assured that they know (subconsciously). Your mind is a parachute

2- Fear of the unknown

Fear of the unknown is the cancer that has plagued our society for many, many generations. And that is because of a lack of knowledge. Not that the knowledge is not available, but that people are refusing to search for it, also many that are faced with truth/knowledge, they ignore it as if they could get away from it. Searching and finding out knowledge will make a person feel responsible and they would have to act on it. Unfortunately, most people don't want responsibility, they want a comfortable life. Everyone wants a comfortable life, but I have a few questions for you:

How does life become comfortable?
What is required for comfort to arrive?
Is comfort coming from somewhere or is it already present?

"To live a comfortable life, you must live it uncomfortably"

What this quote means is that you must be engaged with everything you do throughout the day. Engaging by enjoying it, not feeling anything, you do as a chore. By putting yourself in action for everything, on the surface it looks uncomfortable because of laziness.
But when you enjoy life, when you appreciate every life form, when you are grateful for this beautiful world, then it becomes a play where you have fun. So, it is an uncomfortable life at the beginning or until you realize this amazing little secret where everything you do and everything you say is a

radiant beauty that will shine all around you.

> *"When you spread positivity, love, light, and gratitude, you will get that back tenfold as your behavior, your way of life will affect everyone and everything around you, even a blade of grass will be affected by your choices."*

Not having knowledge is no different than having knowledge but not applying it. Both groups are part of ignorance. And we all paid for it, from our parents, our parents from their parents and so on.

> *"If a man is born ignorant, to parents that are ignorant, in a society that is ignorant, lives a life of ignorance, then ignorance becomes the norm. Thus, indoctrination can be called education, hypnotism can be called entertainment, criminals can be called leaders, and lies can be called Truth, because his mind was never truly his own" -Gavin Nascimento*

But that doesn't mean that we can remain ignorant. We have full capability to create our own destiny. We are not destined to suffer because of the past. You can break the curse by shining the light toward the path to enlightenment instead of wandering around through the distractions that are off the path. One of many distractions is "worry." It is unnecessary. You only lose by worrying. The main worry that humanity has is that of other people's opinions. Just know that:

> *"What other people think of you is only a reflection of who they are. Why worry about someone that you don't know? That unknown (the supposed you) person that you don't know, is only known to them. They only know what they created in their mind." -S. K.*

So why worry?
Break a mirror (you don't have to break it, I'm sure you have enough imagination to make this work out) and go in front of it, what do you see?
Do you see yourself?
Do you see the one that you think is you?
Or do you think that an unknown person has taken hostage the real you?

Worrying is meaningless, not only that you don't gain anything, but you lose big time. Be a lion and don't waste time worrying what sheep think or say about you. What they say or think about you is only a reflection of themselves that they see on a distorted mirror. There is a difference between judging and observing someone. Judging is a poor word. You can simply analyze someone, and let's say you talk about that someone with a friend of yours.

Talking about it may spring a philosophical conversation about life that you and your friend can learn.

In this case it would not be judging but observing that person and at the same time respecting him/her for existing and being available (directly and indirectly) for you to cause a philosophical/moral conversation. But if you look down on that person and compare yourself by boosting about your height, your intelligence, or anything else for that matter, then it would be judging. As you or I are not above anyone. **Embrace all emotions and transmute them into bliss.**

> *"Do not fight against pain, do not fight against irritation or jealousy. Embrace them with great tenderness, as though you were embracing a little baby. Your anger is yourself, and you should not be violent toward it. The same thing goes for all your emotions" -Thich Nhat Hanh*

Clear your mind, heart, body. Do not end up becoming a demoralized person. A person that is demoralized is unable to assess true information. Exposure to information does not matter anymore to a demoralized person. The facts tell him nothing, even if you shower him with information: with authentic proof, with documents and pictures. He will refuse to believe it. To be demoralized is a tragedy. You that are reading this are not demoralized.

Our beautiful planet (and everything that comes with it, yes Gaia is a female, our spiritual mother), has been in a spiritual warfare for roughly 27000 years. The controllers/dark side have no power, they are not part of the Source (the source that all of us humans have come from).

Whatever power they have is what you let them have. Because majority of people don't innerstand the Universal Laws, people create unknowingly suffering and misery against themselves. And this benefits those that crave control over others. So, how did we end up here? The dark side (or Evil ones as we'd like to call them, although their dark, nefarious actions are results of our ignorance), had one advantage over us and that was their innerstanding of energy.

After the fall of Atlantis, humanity was knocked down into an amnesia/deep sleep state that allowed the dark forces to move in and take control of every aspect of human's lives. Their awareness/knowledge of energy was hidden from the Collective so they would not recall that they are in fact the ones who hold the power. We are descendants of the 1st civilization after the fall of Atlantis. The only reason that the Matrix is still standing, barely, is because it exists within each person's EGO mind.

By inserting fear into our consciousness, belief systems were created, and these belief systems shape the way you see reality. We are all part of

Source; therefore, we hold the power to create. We hold the power to freedom. Humanity was manipulated into creating their own hell and the Dark one's Heaven.

Over 99% of beings on this planet unconsciously serve the controllers, the darkness and the illusion on a daily basis and have no idea that they are doing it. Manipulation, whether from others or your own doing is still you that contributed to other people manipulating you. Nobody can manipulate you unless you give them permission to. In the case of others manipulating you, it was not an active consent, it was an unconscious consent.

But it's you that allowed it, nonetheless. Fear and insecurities are the main causes that make you an easy to manipulate human. And the worst of all EGO, the lower self, the illusion that covers the real YOU.

No matter at what stage in life, we think we know a lot. Yes, we learn a lot more than before, assuming what we learned are truths. But in the grand scheme of things, we have not learned anything, we are still in the new-born stage in life.

In one of the interviews with the great mystic OSHO when he was asked what he had learned all life through personal experience and by having read thousands of books? I'm paraphrasing what he said. Osho replied:

"After reading thousands of books I can tell you with certainty that I realized that I know nothing"

Do you recognize these 12 invisible enemies?

Arrogance

Lust

Low Self-Esteem

Anger

Grudge

Cheating

Greed

Conceit

Hate

Lying

Selfishness

Gossip

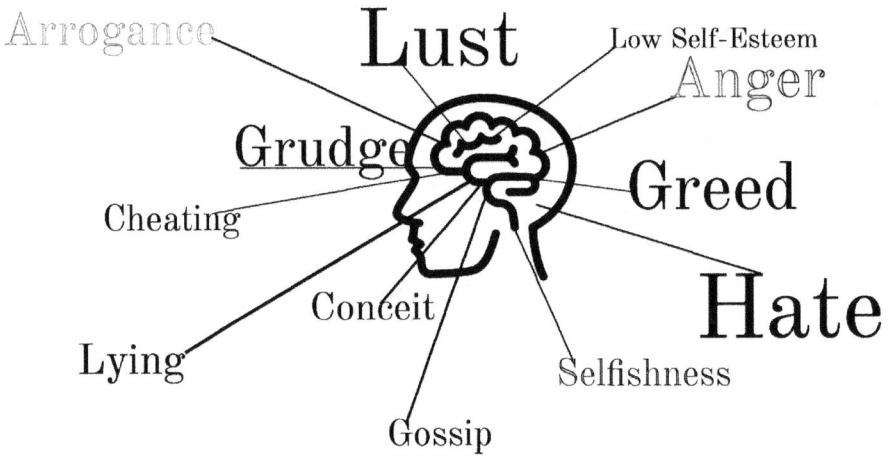

Why invisible? Because they don't exist. They are all illusions, or distorted truths. They exist only as a result of people not following the Universal Laws which you will read about them later. How do you manipulate others or yourself? Directly or indirectly. The answer is that you gave the tools of creation to external things or people. Since everything is energy, anyone or anything can be manipulated for good or for evil.

"By not knowing yourself, your thoughts and actions can build a bridge without foundation." -S.K

And that foundation is knowledge and innerstanding. You cannot have innerstanding without knowledge. If you only have knowledge, it does not automatically mean that you have innerstanding. To innerstand something, you have to put the knowledge in practice. The first step to gain wisdom is done by practicing knowledge from the observer point of view without you getting invested emotionally toward people or things. There is no reason why we humans shouldn't be living in harmony with each other. But why don't we? Is it really the 12 enemies above or is there a hidden hand that shakes us where we find ourselves in a soup of stirred emotions? Here is a small analogy about the hidden enemy hand.

If you put in a jar 100 black ants and red ants, nothing will happen. But if you shake the jar, ants will start killing each other. Red ants will believe black ants are the enemy, while black ants believe red is the enemy. The truth is that the real enemy is the person that shook the jar. It is the same thing in our society. There is a hidden hand (a group of people/entities) that pulls the strings.

The strings are the enemies (your emotions). How are your emotions triggered? By racism, social status, news (FAKE) media, tv shows, magazines etc. They all trigger and weaken your psyche. We may look different from the outside, but we are all the same inside as the outside appearance is just the makeup that covers the REAL US, the multidimensional beings that we are.

Seduce your enemies so you can welcome with open arms your friends. By eliminating/subduing your emotional enemies, you cannot be manipulated anymore as you will be all powerful. When you practice observational routines regularly, your mind becomes clear. And do you know what happens to the 12 enemies when your mind is clear?

THEY DISAPPEAR

Technically the enemies were never there. You projected them from your mind. When you spend your mind on a vacation, your treasure chamber becomes healthy and functions properly. All those negative low vibrational enemies can be replaced with your best friends mentioned below.

Now, say "hi" to your **best friends**

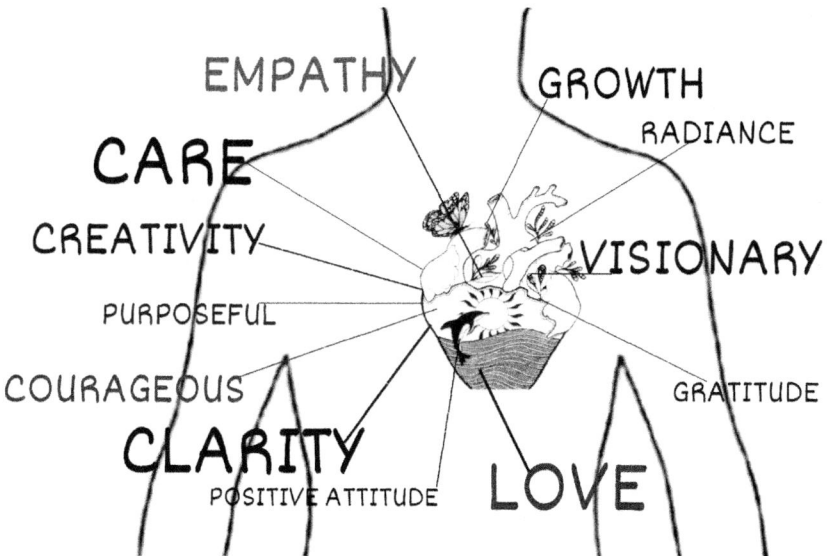

EMPATHY   GROWTH

RADIANCE

CARE

CREATIVITY

VISIONARY

PURPOSEFUL

COURAGEOUS

GRATITUDE

CLARITY

POSITIVE ATTITUDE   LOVE

"Before waking up your friends from deep sleep, make sure first that your enemies are accompanied outside of your castle forever."

SAIMIRKERCANAJ

Chapter **THREE**

YOU ARE VERY IMPORTANT
TO THE UNI-VERSE

Make no mistake, do not become arrogant, as other things are even as important as you, such as animals, plants, trees, bugs, and bees. Bees are one of the most important species of Earth's pollinators. They support the production of food crops worldwide. Insects-pollinators are integral to a healthy environment and the planet's survival.

According to the international conservation non-profit Earth watch Institute, bees are the most important species on Earth. Without bees, global food production would look very different. Three out of four crops that produce fruit or seeds for human consumption depend at least in part on pollinators. While pollinators also include bats and birds, insects such as bees, butterflies and hoverflies are the most common. Pollinators support the production of 87% of leading food crops worldwide. It's not just one species of bees that supports global agriculture production.

Honeybees may provide up to 14% of global pollination services. But bumblebees and other wild species represent most pollinators. So, as you can see, you are not the most important species on this beautiful Earth. We all are important to each other. When we become arrogant, we treat each other badly, our mind gets confused and conditioned for survival of the fittest which in turn results in the destruction of our happiness.

Arrogance breeds destruction as a result of ignorance. Be one with everything. Everything has a consciousness, even a rock, low consciousness but a consciousness, nonetheless. Because a rock doesn't move it doesn't mean that it doesn't have a consciousness. Everything is energy. Everything vibrates but at a different level of frequency.

We humans vibrate (the atoms) at certain speed that makes us look physical like humans. Other species, or plants, trees also vibrate at certain frequency speed. Just like you look externally different from your friend, co-worker, or

anyone else, also we as a species look different than another species.
You are the child of the Universe. The child that was always loved, and always will. Live in peace with all other children of the universe.

"The universe is saying" Allow me to flow through you unrestricted, and you will see the greatest MAGIC you have ever seen"

Chapter FOUR

IS AGE JUST A TRIP OR A TRAP?

Instead of saying that you are let's say 35 years old, I greatly suggest you say that you have travelled 35 times around the sun. Trips don't end but years do, as in our 3d physical life perspective. I went into a lot more details about why we age in my previous book "**I AM THE KEY THAT OPENS ALL DOORS.**" Every holiday (**HELL**yday) is not what you think it is. Just a simple birthday celebration is a satanic ritual whether you realize it, whether you believe it or not.

A birthday is a satanic ritual about chanting around a flaming object (cake) that represents the number of years taken off your life, upon which the flames are blown out and a knife is stabbed through it. Do you now innerstand what people do when they celebrate their own death? They unknowingly celebrate their own destruction. Since our society has been conditioned to think that life is only what you see or touch, anything immaterial is dismissed. Being destroyed internally-emotionally/mentally and spiritually is way more detrimental than being destroyed physically.

Picture yourself bleeding every time you celebrate your birthday, would you keep doing it? Of course not. While you think that you are feeling good, your inner YOU bleed every time. You must realize how powerful you are, and you can touch the sky.

> *"You have the power to be and do anything. You are both the poison and the cure. The difference between happiness and unhappiness lies in the quality of the thoughts. You can plant and take care of the roots, or let the roots rotten and water the leaves by hoping to save the plant"*

When people ask me about my age, I don't reveal it? Why? Because is detrimental to my inner biology. I don't like aging therefore I don't keep it in my consciousness. Anything that you keep in your consciousness, it becomes **THE NEW YOU**. If you think that you are aging, then you are aging, regardless of what the number of your age is. I have seen countless of times very young people feeling tired, lazy, and saying they feel so old, while being in their 20s. It is a madness to think that. They are already defeated by their own be**LIE**fs.

AS YOU BELIEVE, SO SHALL IT BE.

This is one of the major Natural Laws which you will read and innerstand in the section Natural Laws. I believe that I am 25 y young. In the documents says otherwise but I choose this number. I choose my age. I reprogram my cells. Don't get offended when someone asks about your age. Either say the truth and admit what/who you are or pick a number so you can reprogram yourself for life and not for death.

I mean to pick a younger number for the reason of reprograming your subconscious, and not to feel better temporary while at the same time you feel depressed from getting older. You cannot trick the NATURAL LAWS. They are unchangeable. Many women get triggered or offended when someone asks them about their age. Why? Think about it. It has bad implications for mental and emotional health. By getting triggered, first they give their emotional power away and secondly their values are diminished.

Their values are not really diminished but in their perception they are. And third by not wanting to show their age, automatically their perception dictates their inner biology to prepare for death/premature aging. That's the science of Epigenetics, but I'm not going to write about that in this book. I elaborated on my previous book about why we age so I won't be repetitive here for those that already read it.

Age can be either a TRIP or a TRAP depending on your way of thinking. Trips are unlimited but traps end your life. Who set the trap? You did.

How?
By focusing your attention on numbers (birthdays every year), by beLIEving that based on outside appearance, it defines someone's age, therefore, you think you are getting older. The more you think about something, the more you bring it into your consciousness, and it becomes part of you. When you identify yourself with your age, your external appearance, you get further from the destination. Your outside look is like the leaves of a tree.

The leaves change colour, wither, fall. So does your physical body, it changes, it wrinkles. The roots of the tree are eternal and never changing. In case you did not know, the trees that you see everywhere as apart from each other, are not separated at all. Their roots all are connected to each other energetically. So is you (your soul), your energetic you is connected to every other human (including me).

My point is that your external is not as important as who you truly are on a metaphysical level. The body withers and dies, but not the soul. If you focus on a spiritual path, by being in alignment with your inner self, then your physical body will/should stay young for a long time as you wouldn't bombard your cells with self-destructive thoughts and emotions.

Why?
Because of having given part of the brain so that the 12 enemies take residence in it. Those enemies are enforced even more when you associate with those that have not realized yet what their path is. This is what you must innerstand that because you and your friends or family members operate within a circle, it doesn't mean that you have to stay in that circle. If people hold you down and not empower you, then they have cornered you in a cage/circle.

Get out of the circle by losing your mind, and I mean the mind that others gave you. Because your mind is full of memories, complaints, drama etc from all kinds of people. Let them go peacefully and focus only on your inner peace, it's when Magic happens, when you discover peace of mind by letting go those that have no idea who they are.

Only the sky is the limit. You have the power to be and do anything. You are both the poison and the cure. The difference between happiness and unhappiness lies in the quality of the thoughts. You can plant and take care of the roots, or let the roots rotten and water the leaves by hoping to save the plant.

ACKNOWLEDGE IF YOU WANT TO BE ACKNOWLEDGED

If you acknowledge evil, then you are already on your way to enlightenment. That's why most people choose to deny it because it is more comfortable. Acknowledging something that requires you to do something about it, takes effort. Your moral compass will rise toward innerstanding, love, compassion, gratitude, and freedom. Ignoring the outside reality without having it innerstood yet, it won't magically make it disappear, as you are part of that reality. You did your part to create it.

So, if you contribute to its destruction, you must also work on the reversal of it. You might say that you didn't destroy the world because you were a law-abiding citizen, paid your taxes etc. My answer is: Do you know what being a citizen means? It means that you work for a corporation called (insert the country you are a citizen of). Which means you are 100% responsible for any decision that the government makes. You paid taxes, to whom? What for? Do you even know where your taxes go? I have bad news for you, they don't go to build roads, schools etc.

They are invested for nefarious reasons. Before there were any taxes, we already had roads, schools, railroads etc. At least in the most developed countries. So, you see, by not knowing that you are part of a corporation you did your part in the destruction of our system, as did I because I didn't know any better. But when you know, you cannot ignore it anymore.

Knowledge is a gift. When someone gives you a gift (in this case "knowledge"), a lot more is required of you. -Action- You must invest yourself in this play called "**LIFE.**" Be active and creative in every step of your life, as that way creator/universe will acknowledge you. Not that it doesn't because you wouldn't be existing if Creator didn't acknowledge your existence. I mean that the Universe will dance with you when you are in alignment with it. It will be a magical union dance that will bring you bliss.

You can't just ignore life. You are in the middle of it. You are the seed. You must water the seed if you want the tree (you) to produce healthy fruit (a life of empowerment, love, gratefulness, peace, freedom and prosperity).

Chapter **FIVE**

DESIRES ARE THE CHAINS OF
YOUR IMPRISONMENT

W hat are desires? Desires are states of mind and are expressed in terms like wanting, wishing, longing, or craving - These are chains that have made prisoners of humanity for many thousands of years.

"There are three kinds of people: Those that know themselves, those that think they know themselves and those that have no clue who they are."

How can your heart meet God when it is chained by desires? The biggest desire that all humans have is to connect with another person. Meaning love and be loved. A desire for love is not a problem **ONLY** when both you and the person you love vibrate in the highest vibration that there is, which is unconditional love toward all things and people. That kind of vibration is of 9th dimension. Earth can support up to nine dimensions.

The 9th vibration one is the vibration/frequency of LOVE. Materialistic things are desires/attachments also. People in general can be attachments. You don't need to be in love to desire someone. You may desire someone that INNERstand and listens to your problem. But this kind of desire is an attachment.

"If you rely on someone else to make you feel good, you plant the seed of inner destruction, instead of digging deep in your heart and ripping off any weed that may have sprouted"-S.K.

All desires and attachments are by products of you being distracted by the past and the supposed future. If you are present, then you will not desire anyone or anything. You might ask me as you should:

"But Saimir, we are human beings, we have desires, and desires are beautiful especially when in Love."

Yes, that is true, but how much suffering desires bring? The problems derive when two people are misaligned. For the desire to be genuine and constant, the heart and the mind have to be resonating. A thing that I'd like to remind you is that the mind and brain are two different things. The brain is just the physical tool that makes your thoughts visible. The mind is invisible.

The mind is immaterial. Your mind is like a droplet in the ocean of the universal/supreme mind. As above, so below can be used in this situation where your mind/higher self is above, and you (yourself when conscious) is below.

The main reason why people fall for the desires is that they don't innerstand the **UNIVERSAL LAWS**. Later on, you will see how the Universal laws work. If you follow them, you can have anything you want. I don't seek money, therefore, I have enough to survive. You may want lots of money, and you can have it when following one of the laws. But be careful that if your desire for money damages another person, you create bad karma, and you will initiate the Law of Consequences (one of the Universal Laws).

Money doesn't bring happiness. Happiness comes when you innerstand that we all are one. If you think you are separate from anyone else then, the laws will work against you. Be careful what you wish for. Be always aware that you're a fragment of God, the Universe. **We all are God's children**. If one of your children was mean and selfish to your other children, would you do anything about it? Of course, you would as all your children must be loved equally. If you don't love all your children equally, then you have fallen for the man-made laws and strayed away from the Creator's laws.

Desiring a person without having the knowledge of the laws, you will create unpleasantness in the long run. There is no way that you can be 100% successful about a certain subject if you have no knowledge of the UNIVERSAL LAWS. And of course, by not having knowledge and innerstanding of the universal laws, besides desires you will create attachments, which a desire usually ends in an attachment anyway.

Learn and practice the LAWS. They require commitment and an ongoing effort. You can't expect change by staying in the same spot. Practice detachment. When you do that, it will be much easier to withdraw yourself from any desires, any relationship or any other attachment be it a person or thing.

Desires are so tempting that almost everyone falls for them. Well, the ones that are controlled by the lower chakras (energy centers). But, it doesn't have to be difficult to not have any desires. At least not having any major one which it can bring suffering in the end. Become disciplined enough to withdraw from any temptations, whether by your own thinking or by other people. You can do it. But only when you practice the universal laws.

One more thing about DESIRE.

Do not have one-night stands (casual sex), or sex without love. Many people fall (rise) in love after a good sex (casual). This is because the heart chakras are connected to the genitals. Meaningless sex depletes the life-force and damages the heart chakra (LOVE center)

That's good if it turned out to rise in love with someone you resonate which chances are very slim. And it is ok if you rise in love and shortly doesn't work out. But the big problem is if you have children with that person, you cannot undo a creation. Therefore, it is best to refrain from casual sex, take as time as you need until the one to be the best fit for you appears.

Do you know yourself?
Do you think you know yourself?
Do you have a clue of who you truly are?

YOU ARE.....?

Chapter **SIX**

SILENCE, THE SNOWBALL EFFECT

"Hang around with your best friend SILENCE, and you will give the answer to anyone who rejects or doesn't value your words. Transmute silence into LOUD empowerment." -S.K.

As you may already know or innerstand, silence can be the biggest sound. Not necessarily immediately or audibly. Being silent translates to also making a sound. Hmm, how is it possible? First, that you cannot hear everything, it does not mean that everything cannot be heard.

We as humans are programmed to see and hear within a certain frequency range. One of the reasons for that is that if you could hear or see everything in all dimensions, or even in the same dimension that we are living but at a further distance, let's say 5km away, you would go crazy, you would not be able to function.

Our brain is set to compute a limited number of things per day. It doesn't mean that we cannot hear or see way more than what is possible. What is possible has to do with our species that has been programmed to operate within the 2 DNA strands' capabilities. We are being upgraded in real time now. We are being upgraded to operate with twelve strands of DNA as we were originally intended to, but unfortunately the extra ten strands of DNA that are not active yet, were deactivated by another species that genetically modified us a long time ago for the purpose of controlling us. And their reign over us is ending. We are in the **apocalypse** now.

Apocalypse means simply from Greek 'the unveiling' or the 'revealing of truth'. To go back to how silence can be a big sound. As an example: Let's say that a friend or family member is pushing your buttons/annoying you, and you say nothing whether to not create an unpleasant situation or because you deem it not worth it to waste energy into the situation. Your silence equals as you are saying:

    ONE- *Keep pushing my buttons because I am weak and cannot confront you with logic and common sense.*

TWO- *I know my values, I love myself and I innerstand that everyone that does or says anything, it has nothing to do with me but with a version of me that they have created in their own mind.*

So, as you can see. Your silence can create a big sound (indirectly or directly) in both situations. In the first one your silence will create a snowball effect that more and more people will treat you based on their own versions of you that they have in their mind. How many people do you know in your life? A lot, so imagine if you had to be passive and close your heart and mind to not be disliked or not being strong enough to confront? You don't have to necessarily confront. A good way is to ignore people.

This may sound as a negative thing to do but you are only responsible for your own life (except for when you have little children). Ignoring, resolves half of the problems except for when somethings must be confronted. But most of the problems we have, have nothing to do with other people or things, it has to do with how we react/not react to those things or people. There are times when we must react, and others when we must not react.

And to know when to react or not react is to pay attention to what feels right or wrong. If you confront someone, will it bring peace of heart and mind to you? Will you progress as a result of debating with someone that will bring knowledge and innerstanding to you or to whomever you are debating with? You are the best judge for when to act or not in any situation.

Listening to others on a regular basis will not resolve anything as anyone inner stands from their level of consciousness/innerstanding based on knowledge and putting their knowledge to practice. **Knowledge + Practice = Wisdom**. Now, it doesn't mean that you cannot learn or absorb any lesson from someone else.

Yes, you can but as long as the other person has no attachments (feeling/emotions) toward you as by being attached to you that person's judgment toward you will already be compromised. If I may give you some advice, if you need to vent about an unpleasant situation, just talk with someone that doesn't know any of your private life problems.

As that person will have no attachment or memories toward you or anyone else's that is part of your life. Better to talk with a stranger than with a family member or a friend. My advice only applies when you are surrounded by people that put you down (condescending you), and when you don't feel strong minded. And when you deal with ignorant people. By ignorant I mean those that don't have enough knowledge about giving you an educated opinion. I have seen countless people getting supposed advice from those that have no clue about health or relationships.

As one example, a co-worker of mine that I used to work with, was very fat and a very nice person. She was giving health advice to her friend that was in a very fragile situation based on her private life problems. And by being in a weak health state (not the fat one), her logic/common sense was compromised and was ready to do what the other unhealthy person (the fat one) suggested.

So, I had to take both of them separately and explain/suggest how to be healthy, at least healthy enough to the point that the body fixes itself and does not need medications. The fat person's intention was good, it is what she knew, she didn't know any better. My point is no matter who you talk to about any problem you may have, you are the one to decide in the end.

Have you ever heard the saying **"Measure 10 times but cut once**?" Which means ask/talk to 10 people and you yourself decide what to do about a problem at any given time. Ten different people might give you 10 opinions, and I may be the 11th one. But you can learn from all. Even from someone that doesn't know what he is talking about, you can learn to discern and be careful when you listen to someone that doesn't know anything of value for you. It doesn't mean that you need to be selfish and collect things that are of value to you by disregarding others.

Just be grateful for anyone's opinion. Remember that right now you can give an educated opinion to someone that is at a level that you were 5 or 10 years ago. Learn all the time from anyone. But to be in a position that you can learn properly you have to have a healthy mind, body, and soul. Your soul will not be healthy if you have a busy/crowded/unhealthy mind/body. Previously I used the word fat a couple of times.

There is nothing wrong with the word fat. It is wrong only when you think so, but it applies only to you and not bleeding on others as a reaction of your life's perception.

Would you rather be lied with nice words that make you feel good temporary and keep you a slave chained by your own thoughts/expectations?

Or

Would you rather someone speaks the truth which then you have a big chance to make progress in all areas in life?

Should have I used the words not skinny? You decide what word should be used. If you do have an opinion about the words that need to be used, then you are creating a big sound by your silence. It is a silence because you will not actually tell me that as you won't meet me in person, unless you are someone that knows me personally. If you indeed are someone that knows me personally, then I have a ready answer for whatever you throw at me;).

Thoughts are sounds. Every thought you have you create an internal sound in the form of suffering in your mind or heart, or an external sound by getting triggered and saying words to anyone that triggers you. The internal or external sound as a reaction to your silence are not just negative but can also be positive ones. Based on your self-values, critical thinking and the more important thing is based on if you innerstand that the difference between happiness and unhappiness derives from the things you can or cannot control. The moment you invest energy on things you cannot control, is the moment you are one step forward toward the grave.

Your aim should be toward having peace of mind and heart. That's like winning the universal lottery. By hanging around with your best friend SILENCE, you've already obtained the answer to anyone who rejects or doesn't value your words. Transmute the silence into empowerment. Would you **DESTROY** with your silence, or would you **BUILD**?

chapter SEVEN

INNER PEACE IS PRICELESS

No amount of money or possessions will fill your heart. Heart operates in high Love frequency. Money and materialistic things belong in the low vibratory dimension which is where humanity is at right now as it has been for a long time, but it is soon all ending as we are entering the Age of Aquarius, the age of Love and peace for all.

Why is hell so awful? One, it was created for Satan and his demons. Secondly, because people don't realize that hell is the absence of God.

There's no air in hell...because God is a breath of life.
There is no peace in hell...because God is the prince of peace. There is no comfort in hell...because God is the comforter.
There is no love in hell...because God is love.
Hell is darkness...because God is the light.
You don't have to go there!

The above section is metaphorical. Hell, or Heaven are not actual places where you can go, they are states of mind. You are both Heaven and Hell. You have all the power to choose Light or absence of it. But there is only one way to escape it and that is through Christ Consciousness that is within you and everyone else. Nobody can save you but YOU.

"Do not let behavior of others destroy your inner peace" -Dalai Lama

All of us have another stubborn animal within, the chattering monkey as the Taoists call it. It is the nonstop talking mind, that rascal that won't stay in one place. All of us go through hard times but those hard times are lessons and not mistakes. It's when most make the mistake of thinking that the hard times are mistakes.

There are going to be very painful moments in your life that will change your entire world in a matter of minutes/hours. These moments will change you. Let them make you stronger, kinder, smarter, humble.

But don't become someone you are not. Be yourself, express yourself genuinely without the need to please others and without the worry of what others will think. Nobody knows you, only YOU know you. No matter how broken you can be, there is always the possibility of undoing what seems impossible. Hold yourself together, keep moving even if you feel like shattering. Keep going, rebuild yourself by fighting the darkness within that keeps you a hostage. In hard times, you must ask yourself:

"What is this teaching me?"

"Instead of blaming things or people, take a step back and be the mirror of your soul, look at it in the face and transmute your soul's tears into laughter."
-S.K

Hard times are blessings in disguise. It is a blessing when you see positives from a negative situation. Learn from a negative hard situation and let go of it. Do not keep it anymore in memory as it will hunt you down and keep you a hostage in the past. Your life was never a mistake if you learned from the past. Well, your life is never a mistake regardless of the circumstances. There are only lessons in life, no mistakes.

Every negative or unpleasant situation that happens in your life is an opportunity to grow and expand your consciousness and develop a healthy mind and subsequently a healthy body. The moment you change perception and see things from the LESSON and not the mistake point of view, it is the moment that you open the magic gate. The gate of success, the gate of total freedom. That's when you have achieved a Godlike level of freedom when you have conquered the darkness within.

"Don't allow the behavior of others destroy your peace of mind"
Then, and ONLY then you will enjoy **INNER PEACE.**

Chapter **EIGHT**

POSSESSIONS AND ATTACHMENTS ARE THE ENEMIES PEACE

Owning things or people is totally wrong. In my point of view, we own nothing. It is just an illusion. Even the body you carry with you everywhere you go is not yours. You have two sides, physical and metaphysical (soul/higher self). You are God (one of its unlimited fragments) experiencing itself through your physical body. Ownership is one of Ego's traits. No matter how much you think you own, it will never ever be enough. Below there is a beautiful meaningful little story of a monk and a wood cutter in the woods.

Once in a village there was a wood cutter that would go to the forest every day to cut wood and then sell it in the market. His income was very low. One day when he was cutting wood in the forest, he saw a monk who was meditating. He approached the monk and sat in front of him. After some time when the monk opened his eyes, the wood cutter asked him:

"O wise one, I am very poor. Please give me a solution for my problem."
The monk replied:

"Go Forward."
Wood cutter believed in the words of the monk and started walking forward. After some time, he reached a sandalwood forest. The wood cutter became very happy. Now, he started selling sandalwood in the market and soon he became rich. One day, in days of happiness he thought:

"Monk told me to go ahead, and I found a forest of sandalwood. I must go to him once again. Maybe he can guide me to something more precious."

Thinking this, the woodcutter went to the forest to meet the monk. The monk was sitting immersed in meditation. After some time when he opened his eyes, the wood cutter asked him:

"O wise one, by your grace I found sandalwood forest. Please give me some more advice"
The monk again replied:

"Go Forward."
The wood cutter went ahead with the advice of the monk. Going a little further he found a gold mine. The woodcutter became wealthier after getting gold from mines. He was living his life happily. After some time, again the woodcutter thought about the monk and went to the forest to see him. The monk was sitting peacefully in meditation. The woodcutter again asked the same question and the monk replied:

"Move Forward"
The woodcutter went ahead with the advice of the monk. Now, he found diamonds, rubies, and pearls. He became super rich and prosperous. He was living life in all the luxuries. But one day woodcutter thought:
"The monk knew so much, he could have been wealthy but still he didn't use any of these precious things, why?"

Wood cutter couldn't think of any reason and at last he decided to visit the monk once again. So, he went to the forest to meet him again. When he met monk, he said:

"O wise one, you told me to go forward, and told me the address of wealth and prosperity. But I have a question, please tell me: "Why don't you become rich by having these things yourself?"

At this monk replied:
"What you are saying is correct, but I have gone further, further than diamonds and rubies. Going forward I have found such a pleasure that compared to which these diamonds and rubies feels equal to mud and clay. I have found that special thing."

Wood cutter got curious and asked:

"What's that? Please tell me."
The monk smiled and replied:

"I have found INNER HAPPINESS which I have found through meditation, and in comparison, to inner happiness, even the biggest pleasures of the world become insignificant."

Hearing this, the wood cutter fell at the feet of the monk and said:
"How foolish a person I am, you have wealth of inner treasure and I kept asking

you for pebbles. Kindly tell me how can I find this inner happiness? I don't know how to meditate, please guide me."

The monk said:
"It is very easy to meditate. Just sit down comfortably and start observing what is going on inside your mind. If there is an experience, don't hold onto it, let it come and go. Keep witnessing your thoughts until your thoughts calm down completely. When there is no experience, no thoughts, then you will be in the state of meditation. Then there will be neither the sight nor the seer, then there will be only a zero (zero-point energy/Source of all creation/God), and in that void of zero the lamp of realization burns."

On hearing this from the monk the woodcutter innerstood that the true happiness is not in the outer wealth and comforts. True happiness is WITHIN us all, we just need to find it. In our life we find that we spend all our life earning outside wealth. But we forget how much treasure lies inside us. We never try to turn inward and find it. We spend our whole life in search of happiness, but we do not know that the ocean of happiness lies inside of all of us. Meditation is the means by which we can surely find the treasure of happiness within. We all should take out some time every day to practice meditation. The treasure will not be found at once.

For achieving this bliss, this eternal treasure you will have to practice a little bit every day. And eventually there will come a time when you do not have to try to meditate because the meditation will start to happen spontaneously. Just need to be patient. Possessions, wealth, and fame are worthless compared to inner peace. This amazing story reminded me of the book "The Alchemist " by Paulo Coelho which has the same message.

What is your aim in life?
What is your purpose?
Are you aiming to achieve anything beyond yourself?
Has ever money or materialistic goods brought you continuous peace?
Would you give up total peace by owning nothing for a temporary pleasure/ gratification?

If you answer "YES" to any of the last three questions, then it means (maybe) that someone is holding a gun in your head forcing you to read this book. Take a deep look at your life, from an observational point of view. And analyze your choices.

Are they moral?
Are they selfish?

Get rid of what is not empowering. Invite in:

freedom,
joy,
honesty,
gratitude,
compassion,
LOVE.

Dig out the wealth that you possess in your heart.

YOU ARE ETERNAL.
You possess
UNLIMITED WEALTH

Chapter NINE

SUBDUE YOUR INNER MONSTER
WITHOUT FIGHTING

As Sun Tzu the Chinese general, military strategist, writer and philosopher said:

"The supreme art of war is to subdue the enemy without fighting."

This, of course, does not apply only in war where soldiers fight against each other supposedly for freedom. They don't know that the fighting is instigated by the controllers, banksters (combination of banker and gangster). Duality is the poison that has imprisoned humanity since the beginning of the time when we fell from grace. Solitude is the answer for anyone who seeks to transcend duality and reconnect with their wholeness. There will always be an attraction, or a pull toward solitude whether consciously or not.

By having not realized or practiced solitude, you are dead inside and thinking that it is beautiful outside. Outside it is beautiful, but that kind of beauty is an illusion and temporary of course. All illusions are temporary. Something temporary is a gratification meant to feed the Ego. Search and act/behave with integrity and you will find the answers and the keys of all doors that lead you to the Source, no matter how much control there is around. "Don't take things personally.

"What people say about you, reflects them and not you. If you take things personally, then you give them the key to your kingdom, and they become the king and you become their servant." -SK

Breathing is one of the secrets to subdue the inner monster/EGO. Inhale for 4 sec or however seconds you need to fill up your lungs, hold the breath for 3-4 seconds and exhale slowly double of the inhale time. Before inhaling, put one hand on the belly and one on the chest and make sure your belly becomes bigger than the chest. This way you know you are breathing with your diaphragm which is the only right way to breathe fully, properly the way mother nature/Source/God intended.

When you are doing breathing exercises make sure to focus on your breathing, being consciously aware of what you are doing without getting distracted by thought or outside visual things. A good way to not be distracted by thoughts when you should be in the moment is to half close your eyes. If you close your eyes fully then your mind will wonder in the past or future. If your eyes are fully open, then the outside environment will distract you. So, that's why the best thing is to practice with your eyes half closed.

Of course, when you are not driving or any other situation where you must be alert and 100% conscious of the surrounding environment. This half-closed eye exercise applies also for meditation, especially for meditation which is unbelievably important to not let your thoughts control you. When you master yourself, you conquer the world without a fight. Develop the ability to observe without evaluating/judging. That's the highest form of intelligence. **By not judging or analyzing, you clear the mind. You cannot progress in life with a foggy mind and a troubled heart**. I am closing this chapter with the master of the art of war Sun Tzu.

"Every battle is won before it is fought."

"Victorious warriors win first and then go to war, while defeated warriors go to war first and then seek to win"

In the above quote by war, I mean (Sun Tzu meant both physical and mental war) conquering yourself, conquering your thoughts and emotions and automatically you will conquer the world. Meaning you will admire and enjoy everything beautiful that the world has to offer without harming anyone. Meaning every action, you take must be of the highest purest intention.

ARTWORKS

By the author

Saimir Kerenxhi

Sarman V.

SA1M1R.K

Saimir K

Chapter **TEN**

YOU HOLD BOTH THE LIGHTER
AND THE CANDLE

When you do not know that you are both the light and the candle, you don't have a purpose. You do have a purpose; I mean that you don't realize your purpose. Without a purpose you are a lost soul wondering in darkness, without realizing that the Light is right in front of you if you just put the effort to open your eyes and realize that Love, Freedom, and Peace is always calling you. You have the power to do anything.

You can even write a book. YES, you can write a book, or learn a musical instrument or anything. I am not above you, what I have (which you also have) is **WILL** and **DETERMINATION**. Do not compare yourself with brand new/not successful authors with famous one.

Being famous (I never want to be) does not mean automatically that the book is good. There are many ways/tricks in the business/corporate world to be famous. There will always be someone that knows, has and innerstand more than you if you compare yourself with others. Except for comparing in the sense that you would like to be motivated.Releasing/publishing a book, is a great achievement/success.

You must always do things first to satisfy/fill your soul.

ATTENTION-In this case satisfaction does not equal desire. Desire is part of the EGO. Your soul is your higher self, your true YOU. People I know scoffed when I wanted to start learning drawing, playing piano, painting, writing a book etc. While they were judging me, I kept going and learned all these things. By learning, I mean decently because learning is never finished. Knowledge and innerstanding is unlimited.

So, what's stopping you from learning anything?

The opinion of others?

Self-doubt?

Laziness?

Not believing in being possible.

Believing that someone is naturally born to be an artist?

Everyone is an artist. The only difference is that successful people have the paints (will, determination) in hand and are using them on a canvas (everyday life), while others have the paints put away. You and only you decide whether to take out the paints buried within and create a painting in the canvas called life. Even something as simple as exercise (the ones I put in this book) can be seen as a play or as a job. Why is a child full of energy and likes to move around? Why when we become adults, we don't have that energy? Because we have put away the natural ingredients/paints that we all possess within.

Saying "sorry" constantly implies that you made a mistake. It is a negative thing for the subconscious. My point is the language that we use. Instead of saying "I'm sorry" it's better to say "I will make sure it doesn't happen again" or "you are right, never thought it that way" etc. Or if you are late at a meeting, instead of apologizing say: "Thank you for being patient." My point is to use positive empowerment language instead of a negative one. English or in general our way of speaking in this supposed modern world is poor. Not poetic at all.

> *"I am intelligent because I know that I am ignorant. Only ignorant think they are intelligent."*

This quote seems like it is conflicting itself, but it is not. Intelligence is not finite. We always learn constantly. When you realize that you are ignorant no matter how much you learn, you progress constantly at a fast pace. When you think that you already know a lot, you will become passive and be disillusioned by your own egoistic trap.

THINGS YOU CAN CONTROL

-Your thoughts
-Your attitude
-Your perspective
-Your beLIEfs
-Who you associate with
-How you interpret situations
-What books you read
-How many risks you take
-How you express your feelings
-How kind you are to others
-How kind or hard you are to yourself
-How often you exercise

-What you eat
-How to breath
-How often you practice gratitude
-How many times you smile
-How many times you laugh
-How to stop worrying
-How to stop getting controlled by the past memories
-How to stop getting controlled by unknown future scenarios
 (thoughts)
-How to practice unconditional love
-How not to judge others or yourself
-How to put effort in doing things you desire
-How to be a deterministic person
-How to let other people's opinion fade away

And many other things that can be under control.

PART THREE

SOUL

**THE SEEN AND THE UNSEEN
ARE ONE AND THE SAME**

There is a light within each one of us.
Though, inextinguishable,
Life's sometimes heavy hand can dim its flame.

Our attention caught up in the day to day,
we may forget our brilliance.

But still it remains, beckoning us BACK.
The brightest fire needing only the tiniest SPARK.

Cosmic KELSEY

Chapter ONE

TWIN FLAME

A twin flame is your equal and opposite double, or another aspect of your higher self, a being which is completely connected with you. Or shall I say, a being who had their origins at the same time as you did. You might say that they manifested at a certain point into individuality. You came from a twin flame combination. So, if you are the feminine aspect of yourself there is a masculine aspect, for lack of a better terminology.

There is a being that is your ideal One aspect of Ascension is that generally you are reconnected with your twin flame essence. The longing to be reconnected with the twin flame, to have the ideal relationship, the ideal love expression, is a very strong drive-in human beings. It is the origin of your drive for a relationship. At some level you are aware that somewhere there must be an ideal relationship because it feels so natural to you.

So, the twin flame is the perfect relationship for you, the being that is most completely aligned with you and is in fact part of you on some level. Many of your twin flame essences are not in physical form currently.

They are working from the ascended state. Some of you have twin flames who you will be reuniting with upon your Ascension. So, if you are having trouble with finding the perfect mate for yourself there may be a very good reason ... he/she may not be here. As you grow spiritually there is something like a magnetic attraction which begins to occur between the twin flames.

As they grow spiritually the magnetic attraction between them draws them together at a certain point. If they are not in physical incarnation the attraction will be completed when the Ascension occurs. The connection on the SOUL level can be an amazing experience.

"True transformation and healing can happen when Twin Flame Souls journey unseparated, together by reflecting back to each other any distress and hurt of their inner state being. The aim is to tear down the veil that has been blocking out LOVE, to be in a state of Harmony, unconditional Love for Self and the Mirror SELF"

If you are connected to your higher self, just tune in to your masculine aspect that is him, learn his energy and connect to him. "COMMAND your **HEART**", to "**MAGNETIZE** your **TWIN SOUL**". If you are a male, then connect to your feminine aspect of her. This cannot be done unless you practice meditation regularly. This is an intense journey; it is NOT anything like any journey in the 3D everyday physical life. Besides the twin flame that you may meet when you ascend and leave behind this realm (3D Earth), your own higher self may be considered your twin flame.

You cannot progress in life unless you align with you higher self which is indeed you at the highest level of innerstanding and loving. When you hear the saying "be yourself" it means to be aligned with your real self, to be living life at the highest purpose by loving all species unconditionally. You meet the right person (not the same person) many times throughout life.

Because you are never the same person, you let the opportunity escape by being deceived from your appearance. You associate yourself as (insert your name, social status, nationality, sport fan etc). All those are illusions that keep you a slave tied to invisible chains. Chains that you provided willingly consciously or unconsciously. As a result, you suffer in the short or long term. But your higher self will always suffer in real time.

You immaterial self, your soul is always with you, inseparable. Yourself that you see in the mirror cannot exist without your immaterial self. But your soul can exist without your physical self, not in this realm though, but in a different dimension/s where physical body is not required.

Chapter **TWO**

UNIVERSAL LAWS

As you may have already guessed, by now you are a multidimensional being. Even if you don't think so consciously, deep within you, you already know it. It is of crucial importance that you innerstand that you have the power to choose your future.

Your future involves the destructive laws of man (Man-Made Laws) and the empowering, destiny achievement laws of the Universe. The man-made laws also control your future, but that control is based on the unknowingness of the REAL LAWS (Universal Laws).

The dark side made the laws (fear-based rules) to control you and not realizing that they are just man-made laws to stop your growth, instead of the Creator's Laws that when followed, you grow exponentially. If you disobey the man-made laws, then you are free to explore the Universal Laws which bring happiness, freedom, and peace to humanity.

The laws of the universe give you the ability to control your own future. These laws will control your future regardless of whether you follow them or not. These laws are UNIVERSAL LAWS. Because they affect everything that happens in this universe that we are part of. The Universal Consciousness of the Creator is always everywhere and absolutely nothing can exist outside of the Creator. What is **CREATOR**? Creator is the conscious energy that everything is created from and the Source of **ALL THAT IS**.

The source of *EVERYTHING*. Everything is in Divine Order. If you don't think so, this chapter will make sure you innerstand it. The fact that you got this far into reading, it means that you are already awake from coma. And if after reading this chapter and book, you still don't believe that everything is in divine order, then you will keep repeating the same mistakes over and over in different forms until you do get it. You have no choice. You will eventually have to respect and follow the universal laws. This is CERTAIN.

"You are the soul of the soul
of the Universe and your name is LOVE" -Rumi

Not many know about these laws because this is HIGHER KNOWLEDGE.

85

These laws were taught in the mystery schools (check glossary page,) where many spiritual teachers, philosophers, artists were initiated such as: Plato, Pythagoras. Manly P. Hall, Yeshua, ST. Germaine and many more. This information is hidden in ancient sacred books and writings. It is the most important information of all time. It was taught for thousands of years in the hidden Mystery Schools. This information was hidden from the masses for a long time for the purpose of control or for the purpose to not give the information yet, to a species that is not ready to innerstand it.

Many Mystery Schools were corrupted by the dark side. This information of the universal Laws was kept hidden because when you discover these laws and gain innerstanding of them, the laws become active in your life and you cannot ignore them anymore as they will dictate your future consciously if you follow them as intended for the greater good, or unconsciously where they could work against you. A good analogy from J. Justice in the book "DNA IN THE SANDS OF TIME" writes:

"when you do not direct/follow the universal laws that you learned, it is just like getting into a car, starting it, putting the transmission into gear, then jumping out and letting the car go wherever it wants to. you started the car, you put it in motion, so you are now responsible for its actions and consequences if you like it or not"

It is the exact thing in the Universal Laws. Learning the Universal Laws is a gift of KNOWLEDGE from CREATOR. When you receive a gift, more will be expected of you. This applies to the Universal Laws and not when you receive a materialistic gift which doesn't mean anything in the grand scheme of things.

The Universal Laws have not been taught because behind the scenes the dark side (SONS OF DARKNESS) have been working tirelessly to prohibit the Laws reaching the masses as it would be the end of them (the SONS OF DARKNESS) if that ever happened, which fortunately for you and unfortunately for them it is happening.

I follow the laws to the best of my ability, and I have been rewarded with peace of mind and heart which is the best wealth. I used the term SONS OF DARKNESS as opposed to 'EVIL' because there is nothing evil coming from the creator. Humans invert GOOD into distorted GOOD (evil).

Those kinds of humans are the SONS OF DARKNESS as their purpose is to take your power away and keep you in the dark. The darkness can disappear when enough light shines on it. The Universal Laws information is like the biggest brightest light bulb. Put them to practice and the dark will disappear and be transmuted into LIGHT. Let's get into the LAWS, shall we?

The two most important Universal Laws are:

1- As you believe, so shall it be.

This law always works, everywhere and for everyone. Anything that you believe, good or bad, will happen. It is how it works. Your thoughts get manifested into physicality when enough focus and energy is concentrated. Let me give you an example. If you believe that you will get cancer or any other disease because your mother or father, has it, then chances of you getting diseased are very high. The more you focus on something, the more you will bring it into reality. You create your reality by your own thoughts. It applies the same when you focus on positivity.

If you think and believe enough that you can learn to play an instrument, become an artist, build a business or anything, then you will bring that into your reality. I can confirm this with 100% accuracy. All Universal Laws are 100% accurate. I can give you another example about this law, but this time for GOOD. This is my 2nd book, and I applied this Law for both my first and this book. The more I was thinking about the book, the more I was talking with people in real life or on social media about it. And the more I was talking about it the more I was feeling and willing to write about it and here I am in my second book.

As for the book, being successful or not has nothing to do with the Law, because success is subjective. This book is a success to me because the Universe responded to me respecting and putting in action the Law. The fact that you are reading it and that got this far, is like the cherry on the cake. But not as in personal satisfaction but as in spreading the LIGHT. If you learned anything important in this book, then you would want to talk and teach someone else. When you teach someone else, then that person will keep teaching others and so on. It is how powerful the Universal Laws are.

Many people refuse to read or learn something that they already know that is important. Do you know why they refuse? Because knowledge requires responsibility to put it in practice. They don't want to do that as it takes effort. They would rather live a so-called comfortable life instead of taking actions, become in charge of their life and expand their horizons.

"By refusing knowledge, you automatically refuse wisdom, as wisdom cannot be had without applying knowledge." - S.K.

To quickly go back to me bringing book writing into reality. I have three friends that were hyped up about book writing. They started writing down notes for whatever book subject they were interested in. For a short while they were talking about it but then they stopped. So, they did not keep that thought/energy long enough for it to manifest into reality. Now, this is a simple example that it won't harm them, or you if you don't feel like writing, or learning a profession etc. Everyone is different (and yet the same), everyone likes to do different things. But it is important to innerstand this Law as it can change your life in all aspects.

My friends (I know for sure) don't practice this Law regularly. Sometimes you may get what you want, and sometimes you may not. But the Law works regardless, only that when it works against you it is because you refused to acknowledge it by not caring or by not knowing about it and not practicing it. Since you read about it in this book (assuming it is the first time you read about it), you cannot ignore it. Now you have full responsibility for this gift I'm giving you through the CREATOR. And more is expected of you.

"I gave you the seed. You are the water, soil, air, and the sun. The road to your enlightenment has just begun" -Saimir kercanaj

Nurture the seed or let it rot. The choice is all yours.

The second important Universal Law is:

2- Whatever you create you experience

You create by your thoughts, words, and actions. Anything you believe to be true or untrue you create it if you hold the thought long enough to be manifested in the material world. If you are not clear minded, you will create many unpleasant situations in your life. And as a result, you will start blaming things or people. Pretty much all of us at one point or another throughout our lives blame others or things for when things don't happen the way we like them to. Why is that?

That is because we don't (now we do) innerstand the laws of the universe. How can you blame someone for what happens to you? You created it. Well, you could say that you are a nice person, and your partner is being mean or disrespectful to you for months or years. Here, I will tell you how it is not her/his fault. It doesn't matter if you believe me or not. This is the universal law; you can't escape it. The first, second or the third time that your partner was being disrespectful to you what did you do?

Did you do something about it? If not, that you created your unpleasant situation, and if you talked about it with him, then how come you were/are still with him? It is again because of you not knowing and innerstanding the Universal Law. You create both pleasant and unpleasant situations in your life by following the law (good situation) or by neglecting the Law (unpleasant).

The universe will not stop functioning until you learn how to apply knowledge in life. The Universe and everything in it is always in constant motion. Your destiny is not written by someone, you write your destiny. Those times where people beLIEved that their destiny is written by someone external, are done. We are in the Age of Knowing (Aquarius) now.

"You create your own future. Oversee your life. To be in charge you must have a clear mind. You cannot apply the Universal Laws with a disturbed mind and heart. The only best, most effective way to be in contact (not physically) with the real you (your higher self/your true self), is through solitude. Meditation is the best cure."

3- Law of action: (CAUSE and EFFECT)

You create or manifest through thinking, believing, acting, and speaking. When you balance these four actions, you become a true creator. Lacking one of these will affect one or the other three. Just as if you are not healthy mentally, it will affect you physically, emotionally, and spiritually. Anything you say or do will have a reaction that will affect people and/or things. So be careful with everything you do or say. Your tongue does not have any bones, but it can break bones. Which means that the word you speak is very powerful. It can destroy or build happiness.

4- Law of attraction:

Like vibrations attract like vibrations. Vibrations can be of a high frequency (Love, Empathy, Compassion, Gratitude etc) or LOW (Hate, Jealousy, Envy, Deception etc). Love attracts Love, Hate attracts Hate, Fear attracts Fear and so on. From my experience and doing a social experiment I gather that most people are searching for their **OTHER HALF**.

First, there is no such thing as the other half. Unless we are talking about the twin flame on the soul/energetic level. You are already WHOLE. The term other half has been created by those that don't have your best interest in mind. By those that don't want you discovering your true potential. And so, by searching their supposed other half, many women or men end up lonely, depressed or with a person that is of a different vibrational frequency which brings them an unhealthy, depressing relationship. This kind of attraction is a result of not knowing and innerstanding the Laws mentioned previously.

"When you know your power. When you know that your thoughts and actions are the pathway to success or failure, then you should be very careful of what to think, say or do. "

You are the Universe; you dictate your destiny. Refrain from seeking external help. You are already the cure. Keep your energies high. Elevate yourself to the highest mountain.

5- Law of consequences:

Every action is a choice. There cannot be a random action because an action needs the initiation of the thought first before manifesting into an action. For every action (cause) there is an equal reaction whether the reaction is visible/instantaneous or not. The reaction (effect) will happen anyway. Every single action that you take throughout your daily life shapes your future. Your existence is a reaction (result/effect) of your parents. Doesn't this mean that your actions will result in consequences not only for you but also for others? -YES- Your actions are all results of your thinking.

But are all your thoughts yours?
To answer that you need to pay attention to your circle. Or a cage.

What people are you hanging around with?

People that impose their mindset/ideologies on you, or people that empower you and let you be free, let you express yourself freely without the need to satisfy their expectations? Distance is your solution to figure out your circle and realize if it is actually a circle or a cage. Remember that if your friends, family etc are pushing you in a corner, or being disrespectful etc, it is still your fault for having initiated first an action or an inaction as a result of not innerstanding how the law works. People will take as much as you let them. Letting=Action, taking (they are taking what you give) = reaction which means CONSEQUENCES.

6- Law of Compensation:

What you give to others, will be given to you. Not only about visual/physical materialistic things, but also unseen/immaterial ones such as: Love, Hate, Deception, Anger, Grudge, Grief etc. As the saying goes: what goes around comes around, or you reap what you sow. Now, you might ask me, which I think you did as I love getting questions :).
"Based on this Law, if someone hates me, why would I hate them back when I don't have hatred in my heart?"

In this case the other person will hate himself because you are not falling for the negative side (not innerstanding how it works) of the law of Consequences. But that person surely will either hate himself and/or get hated by someone else. Since you didn't satisfy his low vibration subconscious request, he will investigate finding someone else to hate and spread his poison and he will definitely find someone of his level of vibration.
    The same applies if someone gives you positiveness and you reject it, assuming you think that person is being fake. You will know if someone is fake/not truthful only when your intuition is high, when your gut feeling is not tainted by the mind. Many people judge someone based on the gossip they heard about that person, and that will automatically put intuition in the back

seat. A person with low or no intuition is a lost soul. The law of compensation will work on your advantage when you know and practice the law of cause and effect and as you believe, so shall it be.

7- Law of harmony:

All laws in the Universe have and will always affect each other. They are all in harmony with each other. If you are not in harmony with someone or a group of people, the Laws are still in harmony with each other. The laws cannot have purpose unless you give them purpose through actions.

The Laws exist and function through your actions or inactions. Have you noticed when two people that are all about complaining, gossip, lying get along with each other? That's because they are in harmony together by practicing (unknowingly) the Law of Consequences and they will have unpleasant consequences which will infringe also the law of Cause and Effect.

They put in effect also the law of AS YOU BELIEVE, SO SHALL IT BE (again out of ignorance) and they will pay for it. The so-called harmony between those two people is temporary or long term, and disharmony and destruction of their life will eventually commence. I'm using the word harmony for the sake of the LAW.

As far as those two people being in harmony, that is an illusion, as just the fact itself that they gossip, hate, and lie about others it grows cancer/poison within their heart because they don't innerstand the Law of **DON'T DO TO OTHERS WHAT YOU DON'T WANT TO BE DONE UNTO YOU.**

This was a simple but accurate example between two people that you don't know. But if you are fragile emotionally and mentally you might fall in the trap if a person that you know (family member, partner etc) is a deceptive person, lying person and especially if there are feelings/emotions involved as that would again put your intuition in the back seat. Someone that knows you, will use your weakness against you so be careful. Practice these laws and those that will be of a lower vibration than you will weed themselves out.

8- Law of Love:

The Law of Love is the fabric of the Cosmos and the glue that holds everything together. The Law of Love allows ALL life forms and ALL things to exist in harmony, in ALL of creation. Without this Law there would be no Life. Not only that our Universe would not exist if it was not created out of pure unconditional Love by the Creator, but even after so long being created, this Universe, in particular our PLANEt that is tainted by hate, it is Love that keeps it going.

It is LOVE that keeps us together and has a purpose for living. Throughout many generations there were people that were vibrating in pure love as to keep us going and not being destroyed as a species. But they were a small number of beings compare to millions of us.

We were heading toward the destruction of our species. Luckily, we are on a different timeline now, as more and more people are vibrating in LOVE frequency. It is contagious. More and more people are making a difference by spreading knowledge, innerstanding and compassion/love as I am doing with this book.

Love yourself
Love all species
Love one another
Love unconditionally
And you will only be **REWARDED**

9- Law of gender:

Balancing the Yin and Yang, masculine, and feminine energies, balancing of positive and negative. The creative force of the Universe is the balance of these opposites. So far, I have elaborated the Laws on a singular level, as if it affected mostly, you the reader. But the same Laws apply collectively. As an example, if you and thousands of other people are scared that a specific event doesn't happen, then by the same Law principles that event will happen or not, depending how strong the collective belief is.

Universe always balances itself out. If humanity destroys nature, and doesn't care about one another, then Earth will get rid of a chunk of humanity or all, depending on the severity. Earth will get rid of humanity or part of it in the form of earthquakes, Tsunamis, Viruses (not man-made).

Although personally I don't believe that a virus exists, only a compromised immune system does. When having a compromised immune system, you can easily die from a flu, a germ, or food that has gone bad a little bit. Might as well call it a virus that killed. The Earthquakes, Tsunamis, Volcanoes etc are the built-up pressure that earth releases as a result of humanity not taking care of it.

We don't need to extract oil from Earth for our machinery as we can use free energy which will eventually be disclosed. The oil from the Earth is Earth's blood, did you know that? If someone kept extracting your blood regularly you would be very weak to the point of dying. There are two reasons why the oil is extracted out of Earth's (GAIA's) body.

One - To keep us working like animals and use machinery, and cars to drive to work, to keep paying for it and keep us under control and powerless, making us think that we are so advanced to be driving cars when using oil to use machinery is barely an advancement.

TWO- to keep Earth in coma and weak. Since oil is Earth's blood, Earth becomes weak and by being weak it cannot keep a high vibrational frequency to support us and empower us to become masters of our sleeves.

But thanks to highly advanced beings that have been working behind the scenes to balance out darkness, we are getting out of the dark and entering the LIGHT.

Thanks also to many of us that have kept the sparkle going for many generations. Technically we all are that sparkle. When you meditate and innerstand that this lifetime is one of many, because we have reincarnated many times, then you will truly see the beauty of being alive, regardless of what situation you may be in. We balance each other.

10- Law of one:

If you think because you look different than someone else, that makes you different, you are greatly mistaken. Your outside appearance is just a thin coat of paint covering the true YOU. We are all ONE. We are all one energy. We are all part of the ONE MIND, we are all from the same SOURCE. We are all part of the Infinite Mind/Prime Creator. Separateness is just an illusion. But it is real (to you) when you believe it. If you don't live your life according to these laws, you become selfish and you separate from your real self. You separate from your potential.

Your potential and abilities get buried deep within when you don't know why you do the things that you do. You may have an idea of why you do the things that you do, but it is an illusion and a cheap way to live life separated from each other. Unite first yourself with your real self and then when you innerstand and are aligned with the real YOU, then you will automatically be united with everyone else of every species.

11- Law of vibration:

There are high vibrations, but there are also low vibrations. High vibrations consume low vibrations. Love and compassion consume fear, anger, revenge, hate, judgement etc. When you have a hateful, negative mindset it will consume you, it will consume Love. Technically it cannot consume what isn't available.

It is how it is translated when you let yourself be consumed by the illusions called attachments/desires/distractions. These will suppress the love that is within you, and when that happens you become lost and to balance it out the Universe will send you someone to undo what you did to yourself.

That someone could be a new friend, a new partner, a new co-workers or even a stranger you meet on the street. It takes a single sentence by someone to change your life. Everything is a vibration. If that someone's sentence toward you is of a genuine loving high vibrational intention, it will enter you and crack open the heart that was closed by the enemies (hate, unhappiness, greed, deceit, ungratefulness, ignorance etc) mentioned in this section and book and it will ignite the sparkle again.

And when you are at the bottom, you can only go up. So, that sparkle will turn into a fire and can never again be put out. Learning and living life according to these Universal laws you can only live-in peace, freedom, and prosperity. Until you innerstand and practice daily these Universal laws, you will be a slave to the ten commandments (fear-based laws). They are manmade laws created by man (Nephilim)to control you. But God's/Universal can only empower and reward you when you follow them.

Chapter THREE

JUST BE YOU

Some roads you need to take alone, no friends, no family, no partner, just you and God that is housed within yourself. It's the only road you have ever really travelled anyway, everyone you met and will meet throughout your life, are just actors playing their part. Some of their script is to empower, lift you up so you can progress, and some others' script is to slow you down, and sway you away from your path, the path to true liberation.

So, be careful in what bunch of flowers you take part in, those that look good but have thorns, or those that blossom from thorns. Which means those that look good but have thorns can/will try to sabotage your entire existence, while the other group has already been to the bottom, has already transmuted darkness into light, which in this case the blossoming from the thorns is the transmutation from dark to light.

Those kinds of people innerstand suffering, therefore they wouldn't want others to go through the same hell they went through. They can only help genuinely without expecting anything in return. You must have a fit body, mind, and soul. And to achieve that 1st you must practice solitude, then associate with those that have already practiced it. That way you empower each other. You will empower each other because you will feel morally obligated to help another human or animal species unconditionally.

"A fit body, a calm mind, a house full of love. These things cannot be bought-they must be earned" - Naval Ravi Kant

Who are you? Can you see or feel yourself? The eye cannot see what the heart can. The eye is myopic, the eye cannot see far because there is fog, always was always will be. You know who is responsible for the fog? The mind, your little (part of the BIG Mind) mind and not the supreme mind/God. But the heart can see crystal clear.

The heart can see beyond any illusioned distance. Your heart is the only thing that can bring you peace. Peace comes when you choose to step towards it. Like any change and transformation in your life, chaos usually precedes stillness. Sometimes we are so used to chaos that stillness is foreign and scary.

We don't want to live in it because we fear it will be taken away. We don't trust it. How can you trust the unknown if you don't know what it is? To innerstand peace first you must know what peace is, you must experience it. But to experience something meaningful, information and innerstanding must work in tandem. And what do you use to innerstand something? You mind, your brain. Your mind can create both happiness and sadness. It's how you perceive things that dictate these two states of mind. You are the creator of those states of mind.

You get to continually come back to your center of your real self and put boundaries around what preserves it. Meditation is a great path to beginning this journey. The journey to absolute personal peace, and this is achieved by being you. The real you without being distracted by outside noise (opinion of others). Your external world will match your internal world and vice versa.

Give yourself permission to love the unconditional way. Find peace in your heart to let go of the past and all the choices you have made when you didn't know what you know today. All the choices that you made that you think were the wrong choices, I would say that those were not wrong choices but choices of how not to do it again. There are no mistakes, but only lessons. You were successful in learning the lesson of how not to make the same choices (not a mistake) again.

Unless you have made the same wrong choices which means that you will keep repeating it unless you learn it. Get clear on the life you want and commit to making the choices that will bring what you ask for. To be yourself when you have been conditioned to be anything else, is the most courageous decision you can ever make. To be yourself, some roads you need to take alone, no friends, no family, no partner but just you and God/Source/Supreme creator or whatever term you feel more comfortable using to describe God.

Find yourself. Finding yourself means rediscovering the true you, that inner innocent untainted child buried within you that was imprisoned because of a lifetime conditioning. You were never lost; you were just distracted from the real path.

BE LOVING

BE KIND

BE HONEST

BE HAPPY

BE GRATEFUL

BE HUMBLE

BE CREATIVE

BE THANKFUL

BE APPRECIATIVE

And above all…

BE YOURSELF

Chapter FOUR

DIVINE UNION

Divine union is a much more sacred dance than we are told. It begins with how we think about each other. The universe constantly listens to every single thought that you have. Every thought is a subtle vibration that doesn't go unheard or unnoticed by the universe.

> *"Every thought you have, express it in action for the betterment of yourself and humanity. If you have a negative thought, make peace with it, and let it go, let it disappear in the wind where it will be recycled and reborn into Light. Let it make space for a fertile ground" -Saimir K.*

Your soul is a mirror of your fertile-infertile heart/mind. When there is mutual agreement between the two (physical and metaphysical) then the two paths become one as intended by CREATOR. It also applies for when there is a union between two different people (different from our physical short-sighted viewpoint as we all are the same person). Being separated (from the Source/Creator) all channels of divinity are closed.

When two people let go of their self-destructive thoughts/actions, a stairway to heaven opens for both where total bliss encompasses the couple, or a single person when the union is between the physical (material) and metaphysical (immaterial) self. Heaven is not up there, but in there, **WITHIN YOU**.

Close your physical eyes and open the spiritual one, the pineal gland, your third eye. And one of the most effective and easier ways to open your third eye is through meditation. You may be thinking that you thought that the tap/fluoridated water, processed foods/negative thinking block/calcify the pineal gland. How can pineal gland open by just meditating? I love when you ask me, as I love to answer.

When you meditate, you have access to all knowledge, to all innerstanding.

By meditating you lose anxiety, stress, fear and so on. So, if YOU ARE NOT anxious, stressed, afraid and when you have KNOWLEDGE and Innerstanding as a result of regular meditation, don't you think that it will be easy for you to not consume bad water, food, be free of attachment, develop self-love, compassion toward all life forms, practice gratitude etc?

Of course, you would, as you would have the knowledge and innerstanding of good and evil. You know? The apple of Adam and Eve (it is a metaphor). Union is sacred. There are only two choices. UNION or SEPARATION. Separation is not really a choice but a refusal to the only choice (UNITY).

◆ ◆ ◆

SEXUAL ENERGY EXCHANGE

Sexual energy exchange is sacred. Consciousness is information. The information can be good or bad, although bad is not an appropriate word to use. I would rather use the words "distorted good," just as darkness can be described as "distorted Light." Consciousness can be empowering and healing or infectious and destructive.

A big amount of consciousness or information is exchanged between partners. Not only that you should not sleep with just anyone, but even if you were thinking of sleeping with someone that you think it's worth it to be together, make sure that it is someone that you would want to spend the rest of your life with. It must be reciprocity; the other person should feel the same. You might think that the chances are very slim for that to happen. If you have this mindset, then of course there will be a slim chance or none. You must believe that that person is already available for you, send that intention and gratefulness for that person being available, even if you don't see any hints or clues around you.

You don't have to worry, you just send the genuine intention, and the universe will make sure to bring him/her to you. There are billions/trillions of calculations as to how things will work out which you, me or any human cannot figure it out as our brain only has a specific capacity. The universe will do its job, but you also must do yours. It is not a one-way relation. Besides having a relation with the opposite sex (I am expressing myself from my sexual orientation point of view), also you and the universe are on a relation, always were and always will be.

Every single second that you draw breath, the whole universe is in motion for that to happen. Remember above when I mentioned that it is a two-way relation? Just like in a relationship between two people where the couple don't innerstand each other, don't respect each other which then the relationship ends up stagnant, struggling or ending, so is your relationship with the universe.

If you don't follow/respect the universal laws, your relationship with the universe/creator will also struggle (you will not feel healthy), suffer (you will get diseased) or the relationship (in 3D physical incarnation) will end (you will die from an unhealthy mind/body lifestyle).

It is very important what person you choose to be with, even if you don't have an intimate relationship, even a single kiss, even being in her/his proximity will/can be detrimental to your health as the DNA and information can be transferred between two people even if they don't touch each other. Do not engage with a person of a lower consciousness as they will bleed negativity, energy stagnancy, lower vibrational traits onto you. If you engage or will engage in sexual acts with someone as in being controlled by sexual urge, you have a long ways to go.

You can just abstain from sex for however long it takes to find a suitable partner. I personally know people that got married or had sex because they were feeling too old and needed to follow the trend and have children and family. How did that work out for them? Not so good (for most of them). **Make sure you have high standards and do not settle for less**. It doesn't mean for you to be cocky and look down on people. It just means that you know your values, you have high self-esteem, you love yourself and all life forms unconditionally.

In this subject unconditionally doesn't mean that you can be with just anyone without conditions (not that you would put any conditions on anyone anyway). It was just a general statement where you appreciate and love all life forms.

Only the universe/creator has conditions, and those conditions are the universal laws such as - As you believe so shall it be - Don't do unto others what you don't want to be done unto you. - The law of cause and effect - The law of reciprocity - The law of love, - The law of action - The law of attraction - The law of harmony and more which you already read about them earlier. These laws are unchangeable, eternal. No man can edit or change them. These conditions by the universe are what all must follow, and heaven is within our grasp. Just as hell is within our grasp if we don't follow these laws.

No need to worry how the laws work, because if we analyze, then we create problems and when we don't have healthy thoughts then we will have unhealthy actions and we will infringe the law of cause and effect.

These laws apply for every single part of our lives, including the sexual energy exchange. If you engage in sexual exchange with an unhealed person, you both build bad karma for each other. You will pay for your actions because of your mistake of knowing the law of cause and effect and disregarding it, and the other person will also build bad karma for not knowing the laws, regardless of who knows or does not know the universal laws. Knowing and doing are two different things.

The above 5-6 sentences were explained in the assumption that you know the universal laws, but the other person you are having sexual energy exchange with, doesn't. Even if you reversed it, would not change much. No excuses for ignorance or bad intentions. Even if you are a good person (everyone thinks is a good person) but you do not act when you should do something to stop injustice, you still accumulate bad karma. The world is constantly in motion, nothing stays the same.

You may think you are the same person when you look at yourself in the mirror, but that is not true at all. Every single day you are a different person. Every day you play a role. Now, it is your choice whether to play the same act over and over and stay on the same grade, or progress higher and get closer to home, closer to who you truly are. To innerstand who you truly are you either become enlightened in solitude or in the presence of someone that vibrates in the frequency of love where it will make you feel as you are together but in solitude (free of attachment).

That would be caused by the wrong sexual energy vibrations released from both partners. When two people's energy doesn't match, then it doesn't matter who had a good intention or not.

> "Sexual energy is also creative energy. When you realize this, you start creating magic" -ledbysource

When men innerstand the benefits of SEMEN RETENTION translating to them being able to fully experience their partner's cosmic orgasm (energetically), then they would only want to aim for that kind of experience. Later on there are two chapters about semen retention.

In the book YOU ARE THE ONE by Pine G. Land, the author says: Men are good at some things; women are good at other things. Both divine qualities of men and women put together, makes the union powerful. Those in power do not want a strong union between women and men, that's why they have feminized men and masculinized women through many different nefarious tactics.

Chapter **FIVE**

YOU ARE THE MOST
SOPHISTICATED TECHNOLOGY

<u>YOU - Based on YOU</u>
HAIR- ANTENA
EARS- SATELLITE
NOSE- SENSOR
EYES- CAMERA
HEART- GENERATOR
BRAIN- MOTHERBOARD
IMMUNE SYSTEM- ANTIVIRUS
PINEAL GLAND- VIRTUAL REALITY

Allll technology is based on the human body. The technology that we have nowadays is the cheap version based of the ULTIMATE technology that is the human biological body. Below are some parts of the human body, explained and a few interesting facts about them.

<u>Hair:</u>
Do you know why natives or in general our ancestors (both women and men) kept their hair long? The reason is that long hair was an outward projection of the nervous system. Acting in the way of human antennae. You are not what you see in the mirror. What you are is all a nervous system. Our hair is responsible for transmitting pertinent information to the rest of the nervous system. People with long hair have greater ability to communicate with the other side of this 3d physical Earth. Kirilian technology has shown the difference in energy fields between those with long and short hair.
I wonder how come in our society there are many women with short hair, who promoted this? (Rhetorical question). Just as many women wear pants, hmm? The reason is to suppress women's power as they hold the key to balance.
Since we are living in a system where masculinity has been prevalent for a long time, then it is common sense that the feminine energy must return.

Just as if we were living in a society where feminine energy was prevalent, then we would have needed masculine energy back for balance.

Ears:
Some facts about the ears.

1- Ears are completely individual just like fingertips.
2- Ears are self-cleaning.
3- Only the outer third of the ear canal produces ear wax (cerumen), which moves outward on tiny hairs as we move our lower jaw to talk or eat.
4- The hearing organ, called the cochlea, has 16,000 microscopic hair cells called stereocilia.
5- The unit used to measure loudness (the decibel) was named after Alexander Graham Bell, the inventor of the telephone.
6- You have 206 bones in your body. The six smallest ones are in your ears. Three in each ear.
7- Inner ear has a direct connection with the brain, and anything happens to the inner ear you may lose your body's equilibrium, so be careful when you use Q-tips to clean your ears. Do not stick it deep (don't think dirty, I can hear your thoughts). Personally, I don't clean my ears, meaning I don't clean up the wax that accumulates. That wax is needed. It protects you. It collects dust, dirt, and other matter, preventing them from getting farther into the ear.
Everyday activities like moving your jaw and chewing help new earwax push old earwax to the ear opening where it flakes off or is washed off during bathing. This is a normal continual process, but sometimes this self-cleaning process fails. The result: a build-up of wax that can partly or fully block the ear canal.
In that case then yes clean them up, but only the excess and again I must repeat that don't push deep with the q-tip so as to not damage the inner ear membrane.
Unless you are using a special tool for cleaning the ear, but by having a tool for that purpose, then you will be inclined to clean them up way more times than needed. And your ears will be prone to infections, and if your ears get infected, your brain most likely will too.

> "There is an inclination for people to want to clean their ears because they believe (or conditioned to beLIEve) earwax is an indication of uncleanliness. This misinformation leads to unsafe ear health habits" -Dr. Seth Schwartz

Sometimes I quote doctors or Scientists (the ones I think are independent or from non-profit organizations) for those that are still fragile and believe an information to be true only when it is said by an official doctor, scientist, teacher etc. As I mentioned somewhere in the book, train yourself to be your own scientist, doctor etc.
Beside washing all your body and head, only 4 areas are really needed to

clean everyday: mouth, armpits, genitals, and anus. Don't clean your ears, but if you do be very careful. Don't be conditioned by advertisements on Tv or when listening to the people you hang out with. Many pay attention to some redundant health things and neglect important ones.

Nose
The nose is a miracle organ. Give nose the props for its extraordinary diverse powers. Not only does it define appearance, but it also performs many vital functions without which humans wouldn't be humans. The nose supplies and conditions the air. It warms and moistens air. The nasal hair traps any particle matter and helps in passing only air to the lungs. It also plays a role in speech.
The nose is an essential part of the body because it gets detrimental if we lose the sense of smell. Imagine if something in your house is burning, and you cant's smell? Very dangerous. Or something not as dangerous is if you wouldn't be able to smell when your baby has pooped. I wish I had lost my sense of smell when my kids were at that stage in life. I'm just kidding.
The nose works both as a respiratory organ and an organ of smell. The receptor of smell are placed in the upper 1/3rd pard of the nasal cavity. The nose is divided into external nose and nasal cavity. The external nose has a skeletal framework, which is partly cartilaginous and partly bony.
The nose also helps in speech modulations, amplifications, and modifications. It helps in pronouncing click consonants and nasal vowels. It is way more complicated of how the nose is composed, its function etc. A whole book can be written about it or any other part of the body.

Here are some interesting facts about the nose:

1- During sneezing, irritants (that cause sneezing) are expelled at a speed of 100 miles per hour (160km/h). It is very important to not hold it when you have to sneeze and not sneeze on purpose by forcibly pushing the air out when you sneeze. If you keep it inside and don't sneeze, you will damage the lungs as at that speed, the air surely will create damage of some kind.
    And you if forcibly sneeze, you may crack a rib, as I have in the past. I used to forcibly sneeze while in workplace by having fun with co-workers. That's what happens when you don't have knowledge of self, you willingly destroy your body. Also, if you have to fart, don't force very hard the gases out as you will damage the internals. As you may very well know, you can't urinate and sneeze at the same time.
    That is precisely because of the speed of the air that is blown out. Just as you can't sneeze with your eyes open. Your eyes would pop out if that was not thought of when we were created.
2- In women, nose grows until the age of 15-17 and for men, until the age of 17-19.
3- There are 14 different nose types found in humans. This was found by

Abraham Tamir, a Ph.D. holder (not that it really matters) and Chemical Engineering professor from Israel. He came to this conclusion by surveying around 1,800 nose images.

4- Nose is the best air filter. Human nostrils are lined up with hair responsible for blocking germs and dust. Grooves in nasal cavities make air swirl like stream currents. This is when inhaled, hair is moistened and warmed so that the sensitive tissues of the lungs can be protected. It is during this filtration process that the mucus lining of the nasal cavity captures cold germs and pollen which cannot be stopped by hair in nostrils.

5- Mucus is produced by human sinuses and nose, and it contains white blood cells and enzymes responsible for fighting infections. What I'm about to write now it is very important. Since now you know that the mucus that the sinuses produce is to fight infections, why would you go to the doctor to suppress this amazing protection ability with drugs that the drug dealer (doctor) provides?

When you have a runny nose, or phlegm it is your body expelling out germs, toxins, bacteria by using the mucus/phlegm. If you suppress this protection mechanism with medications, then any germs, toxins that were going to be expelled, now they will remain in your body.

When you get sick, your nose produces more mucus than usual so it can expel and fight the problem. You don't fight fire with fire. The fact that your body was trying to expel it means that your body is already almost in critical condition. Listen to your body, you are your own best doctor. Mainstream doctors have learned the medication way instead of letting the body heal itself. Of course, there are exception where the infection is that severe that medical intervention is required. That's why you do the best to keep your body healthy.

6- Olfactory nerves from nose have direct connection with the brain. That is why several types of smells can bring memories back.

7- Humans release pheromones – a type of chemical released only in response to sexual attraction. Nasal grooves in nostrils are sites rich in pheromones. Human nose is capable of detecting pheromones of opposite sex. The effect is heightened when you live a healthy lifestyle, are a grateful person, empath and honest as you will also radiate high frequency and attract the right partner.

8- Humans don't smell with nose. It is actually the brain that does the job. The olfactory nerve cells in nose are only responsible for capturing smell and sending them to the brain. It is the brain where smell gets identified.

9- Sense of smell in women is stronger than sense of smell in man. That is maybe why women can easily detect when men are full of ****/chocolate.

10- Humans are capable of smelling feelings like sexual arousal and happiness of their romantic partner as long as the two of them are in close proximity.

11- Female nose becomes hypersensitive when they become pregnant. That is why they develop unusual craving and abnormal taste sense.

12- There are presently over 10 million odor receptors present in the human nose. These receptors are sensitive to odor or scent molecules that travel through or float in the air.

13- Men can smell ovulating women. In fact, both sexes can smell major histocompatibility complexes that appear to be different from their own. This is very important because when a person smells a different MHC in opposite sex and mates, the resulting offspring is born with a stronger immune system.

14- The roof of human mouth is nothing but the floor of nasal cavity.

15- Zinc deficiency can also lead to loss of smelling sense.

Eyes

Just like any other part of the body, also eyes are a magical creation. We don't really appreciate our eyes until something goes wrong.

A few facts about the eyes

1- Eyes start to develop two weeks after you are conceived.

2- To protect our eyes, they are positioned in a hollowed eye socket, while eyebrows prevent sweat dripping into your eyes and eyelashes keep dirt out of your eyes.

3- Only 1/6th of the human eyeball is exposed.

4- The entire length of all the eyelashes shed by a human in their life is over 98feet with each eyelash having a lifespan of about 5 month.

5- Your eyeballs stay the same size from birth to death, while your nose and ears continue to grow.

6- An eye cannot be transplanted. There are more than 1 million nerve fibers that connect each eye to the brain and currently we're not able to reconstruct those connections.

7- An eye is composed of more than 2 million working parts.

8- Corneas are the only tissues that don't have blood.

9- 80% of our memories are determined by what we see.

10- Humans and dogs are the only species known to seek visual cues from another individual's eyes, and dogs only do this when interacting with humans.

11- A fingerprint has 40unique characteristics, but an iris has 256, a reason retina scans are increasingly being used for security purposes.

12- Eyes are the 2nd most complex organ after the brain.

13- "Red eye" occurs in photos because the light from the flash bounces off the back of the eye. The choroid is located behind the retina and is rich in blood vessels, which make it appear red on film.

Heart

The amazing generator that you carry with you at all times. The heart is part of the circulatory system. The main function of your heart is to keep blood that is full of oxygen circulating throughout your body. Heart is crucial to your survival; it is important to keep it healthy with a well-balanced diet and exercise and avoid things that can damage it.

Fun Facts about the heart:

1- Your heart pumps about 2,000 gallons of blood every day.

2- Your heart beats about 115,000 times each day.

3- The average heart is the size of a fist in an adult.

4- The heart can continue beating even when it is disconnected from the body.

5- An electrical system controls the rhythm of your heart. It is called the cardiac conduction system.

6- The fairy fly, which is a kind of wasp, has the smallest heart of any living creature.

7- Whales have the largest heart of any mammal.

8- The human heart weighs less than 1 pound. However, a man's heart, on average is 2 ounces heavier than a woman's heart. Hmm, why is that? Maybe because a man would have hoped that someone that he is familiar with, should have lost the sense of speech? I'm just kidding again. If you didn't get the joke within the bold text, it's ok.

9- A woman's heart beats slightly faster than a man's heart. Maybe because he should be quieter and think twice before saying anything? Here, I balanced it out. MEN 1 – WOMEN 1. It's a tie. (I'm laughing out loud, but don't tell anyone)

10- The beating sound of your heart is caused by the valves of the heart opening and closing.

11- It's possible to have a broken heart. It's called broken heart syndrome and can have similar symptoms as a heart attack. The difference is that a heart attack is from heart disease and broken heart syndrome is caused by a rush of stress hormones from an emotional or physical stress event.

So, if you deal with the loss of a loved one, or loss of someone you loved (or that you thought you loved), deal with it, accept that nothing remains the same, life continues and you won't have to have a heart attack, as the emotional stress will weigh on the physical heart.

12- Laughing is good for your heart. It reduces stress and gives a boost to your immune system.

13- If you stretch out your blood vessels system, it will extend over 60,000 miles.

14- Heart cells stop dividing, which means heart cancer is extremely rare.

15- Men are more likely to have a heart attack than women because the ventricle in the left side of a man's heart receives more electricity than a woman's heart. Also, a man's heart is slightly different that the heart of women.

> *Almost all mammals will have about 1 billion heartbeats in their lifetime. Some have rapid resting heart rates so they use up those 1 billion beats in a few years such as shrews, mice, dogs etc. Others have rates of slow long heartbeats like whales and elephants, so they can live to 100 years or more. But then there are us humans, homo sapiens. We are a bit different. If you take an average heart rate of a human adult to be about 80 beats per minute, and we take the average life expectancy of a modern adult to be 70 to 80 years of age.... We get about 2 to 3 billion heartbeats. We get more than double the amount of life out of every beat from our hearts than any other mammal and so far most other animal species in general. In our modern society most people rush and rush as if they going to achieve anything beyond what matters. The more rushing life you live, the faster you will use your heart beats. Slow down your heart rate. Meditation/solitude is the main key/tool to achieve that.*

Brain

The generator of your thoughts. The motherboard. It takes the first spot as the most complicated organ of the body. The eyes take the second spot. Make sure you take care of the motherboard and that it doesn't go rusty.

Brain fun facts

1- The brain in your head is not your only brain. There is a 2nd brain in your intestines that contains over 100 million of neurons. Gut bacteria are responsible for making over 30 neurotransmitters including 95% of the body's serotonin, the so-called happy molecule. That is why it is important to eat healthy. When you eat healthy food, you will also feal radiant, beautiful, powerful.

2- Our brain crave mental stimulation, sometimes to a fault. Men would rather give themselves electric shock than sit quietly in a room with only their thoughts. This is for those man that are predominantly left-brained. When men become more empathetic, creative, nurturing, then balance will be achieved.

3- The blood-brain barrier protects your brain by preventing many foreign substances in your vascular system from reaching the brain. But the barrier doesn't work perfectly and many substances sneak through, some faster than others. Nicotine rushes into the brain in a mere 7 seconds. Alcohol takes 6 minutes.

4- Of the thousands of thoughts, a person has every day, it's estimated that 70% of this mental chatter is negative-self-critical, pessimistic, and fearful. It is very important to have a healthy mind so you can have healthy thoughts and also healthy words which will result in healthy actions.

5- Memories are shockingly unreliable and change over time. Emotions, cues, context, and frequency of use can all affect how accurately we remember something. This includes flashbulb memories which occur during traumatic events.

6- Your brain's storage capacity is considered virtually unlimited. It doesn't get used up like RAM in your computer.

Immune System

Here is another amazingly created system that makes sure you live long. Your immune system protects you from harmful substances, germs and cell changes that could make you ill. It is made up of various organs, cells, and proteins. Without an immune system, we would have no way to fight harmful things that enter our body from outside or harmful changes that occur inside the body. Think very hard before you decide to get injected (jabbed) with any harmful substances.

The immune system can be activated by a lot of different things that the body doesn't recognize as its own. These are called antigens. Example of antigens include proteins on the surface of bacteria, fungi, and viruses. When the antigens attach to special receptors on the immune cells, a whole series of processes are triggered in the body. Once the body has come in contact with a disease-causing germ for the first time, it usually stores information about the germ and how to fight it.

Then, if it comes into contact with the germ again, it recognizes the germ straight away and can start fighting it faster. So, you do innerstand now that when you feel ill, you must not suppress it with medications as you are not giving the chance to the immune system to do its job. You disrupt its functionality and when the same kind of germs comes in contract again with your body, your immune system has not registered properly the information and you get ill again also because your immune system is not as strong as last time it tried to do its job since you harmed it with medications.

The more medications you take, the more harmful it will be to your immune system. Your immune system will also weaken by fear. If you were not afraid, then why would you take medications. If you took medications because it's what humanity does then it means that you were conditioned, So, you see fear is not real but taught. You cannot heal your body. Your body can heal itself; you just get out of its way by not taking any medications and by not eating any solid food.

When you are ill, your immune system must use its energy to heal you instead of wasting it on the digestive process. When you want to heal, you don't add things in the body. Just plenty of water and you will see how miraculously your body will heal itself. But you must let it run its course. Don't be impatient. Ride the illness (discomfort, usually 1-3 days) out. Your immune system needs germs to practice.

Some Immune system fun facts

1- Specialized blood cells are the immune system's greatest weapon. The most powerful weapon in your immune system are white blood cells, divided in two main types: lymphocytes, which create antigens for specific pathogens and kill them or escort them out of the body; and phagocytes, which ingest harmful bacteria. Many of these immune cells are produced in your bone marrow but also in the spleen, lymph nodes, and thymus.

2- The spleen helps your immune system work. Though you can live without the spleen, the organ lies between stomach and diaphragm, it's better to hang onto it for your immune functions.

3- How friendly you are feeling could be linked to your immune system. From an evolutionary perspective, human's high sociability may have less to do with our bigger brains, and more to do with our immune system's exposure to a greater number of bacteria and other pathogens. Don't be afraid to shake hands or hug. I remember when I use to work for a CORPoration at the time of the pLandemic people would fist or elbow bump. I refused to do that as I trust my immune system. I don't' let the external influences dictate my lifestyle and personal individual health activity.

4- You immune system may recruit unlikely organs, like the appendix into service. The appendix gets a bad reputation as a vestigial organ that does nothing but occasionally go septic and create need for immediate surgery. Appendix may help keep your gut in good shape. According to Gabrielle Belz, professor of molecular immunology the appendix houses symbiotic bacteria that are important for overall gut health-especially after infections wipe out the gut's good microbes.

> 5-   A new therapy for type 1 diabetes tricks the immune system. In those with type 1 diabetes the body attacks its own pancreatic cells, interrupting its normal ability to produce insulin in response to glucose. In 2016 researchers at MIT, in collaboration with Boston's Children's Hospital, successfully designed a new material that allows them to encapsulate and transplant healthy pancreatic "islet" cells into diabetic mice without triggering an immune response. Made from seaweed, the substance is benign enough that the body doesn't react to it, and porous enough to allow the islet cells to be placed in the abdomen of mice, where they restore the pancreatic function. This approach has the potential to provide (humans) diabetics with a new pancreas that is protected from the immune system, which would allow them to control their blood sugar without taking drugs.

Pineal Gland:

The pineal gland is one of the so-called endocrine glands. That is, it is a gland of internal secretion. This gland is not active in most people after the age of 20-21. It begins to atrophy or shrivel up at the age of adolescence. It is no larger than a small English or French pea but being so small does not in any way interfere with its importance. It is an atrophied eye. It has all the parts found in the human eye. Anatomically, it is actually a third eye, but it is inside of the head, cannot see out and therefore, it is blind, a dormant eye. Pineal gland is the seat of the soul.

When opened or decalcified, you can see beyond the physical illusion. Most people's third eye is calcified from harmful food, water (fluoridated one), and from being detached from nature. When you are not aligned with nature, your chakras will be blocked, third eye is one of the chakras. Being mentally relaxed most of the time, you will help your third eye decalcify. The more stressful, anxious, fearful, ungrateful, selfish life that you live the more you deteriorate every part of the body.

If you can think for yourself without getting easily swayed away by external opinion, it means that your pineal gland is not totally calcified. When it is open, you can access many different realms that look and seem just as real as this one. Especially in meditation and in your dreams. That would be a real virtual reality experience.

Facts about Pineal Gland (third eye)

1- The pinecone symbols is one of the most mysterious emblems found in ancient and modern art and architecture including the Buddha's head which is shaped like a pinecone. Its imagery shares spiritual illumination, insight, and transformation.

2- Throughout ancient culture including Babylonia, Egypt, Asia and Greece the pineal gland symbolizes the "Third Eye" that we all possess.

3- This gland is located at the geometric center of the brain, and it is considered the biological third eye.

4- The pineal gland produces melatonin, a serotonin derived hormone which regulates sleep. It is important to sleep in total darkness as this gland is very sensitive and will be disrupted even by the dimmest of light. The less disruption to this gland, the more healing will occur in your body.

5- Hindu tradition teaches followers to awaken the Third Eye by activating their "7 Chakras", although the third eye is considered one of them (the sixth to be precise). In nature as the pinecone ripens, the pinecone slowly opens to release its mature seeds. Just as we learn as spiritual beings our seeds begin to bear fruit.

6- The third eye (pineal gland) is the organ of Supreme Connection. You cannot connect with the Source (where you originally came from) with a closed/calcified pineal gland. Meditation, kundalini chakra energy balancing, yoga, mindfulness, connecting with nature are some of the best tools to open the pineal gland.

The stronger mentally you are the healthier you will be. If you take medications with the first sign of illness, then you have already become weak and you gave your life to the medical system that puts only patches on a problem instead of fixing the root of the problem. You are your own best doctor. Listen to your body. Although you may not realize it, your body talks to you at all times.

These are just a few examples of how advanced you are. But everything including how your blood works, your mechanical function, your organs, any fluids that are needed to oil up your vehicle (body). Healing must be your everyday objective. When you have a healed aura, you will attract a lot of damaged people and they will drain your energy. I'm giving you a wise reminder that it is not your job to heal anyone that comes into your life.

Whether you have a healed aura or not, you will still attract people toward you. You are a magnet. Better to be healed than unhealed. Being unhealed you will only attract unhealed people. A healed person can sense your energetic field so they will know not to waste their energy with you.

But the unhealed person will be attracted to you if you also are unhealed because you will be vibrating on the same energetic level as them.

But if you are healed you will attract both healed and unhealed people and since you are healed you will stay away from the damaged ones and all your energy can be invested toward yourself and those that vibrate in care, love, and compassion. If something is wrong with your computer you would fix it first, before you add anymore files to it, or else you would also corrupt the good files that you already have in it.

The same things apply when you let another person in your life. Whether you or he/she are unhealed you both will be corrupting each other. Your immune system is the antivirus for everything that may go wrong in your system. But the antivirus will not work if it is installed too late to do anything about it. Therefore, clean up your house before inviting visitors. Did I make enough analogies?

Chapter SIX

EMBODY BOTH THE SHADOW
AND THE LIGHT

Being Spiritual doesn't mean to be good, it means to be true. There is no spirituality that doesn't embrace all spheres of human emotions. We are spiritual when we are grounded in all our aspects of being, not denying others. What are you running from, in a hurry? A spiritual person is the one who makes feeling a totally embodied experience. This is the spirituality of emotions: welcoming shadow and light to be whole!

To be spiritually healthy, you must start going within, start with yourself first. Heal your soul before you attempt to heal someone else. How can you heal someone else if you yourself don't know what healing is? It is very common in the very early stages of awakening to have the impulse to want to save others and the world. However, as your consciousness expands you begin to see the interconnectedness of all things.

You recognize that you change the world by changing yourself. When you heal yourself, you heal your soul. Your soul is you; you are your soul. Go in front of the mirror:

What do you see?
Do you see the person in the mirror?
Do you see the reflection of the person in the mirror (your physical body acting as a mirror for that person you see in front of you)?
Do you see the person that you think is you?
Or do you see the real you?
Who do you think is you?
The one you see or the one you think you see?
Look into the eye of the person in the mirror.
How deep can you see?
Close your eyes and visualize all the possibilities of YOUs (plural).

Does God have your back when all fails? We are little creators. Creator gave us a brain, emotions, and spirit. It all fails for those that are imbalanced physically, mentally, emotionally, and spiritually. Trusting yourself equals trusting the creator with the amazing multidimensional body mind and soul that gave you. Say to yourself:

> *"I AM grateful for the creation (human, me) that God created, and I appreciate and trust myself."*

Failing happens to those that don't know themselves, so they rely externally on help without realizing that all they need, they already have it within. "Know Thyself" and all doors of peace, freedom, prosperity will open.

Chapter SEVEN

FRIENDS, FAMILY, AND EVERYONE ELSE ARE ACTORS

There are different stages/phases of awakening. You open the eyes from the night sleep, you begin to get your senses back. Then you get up, do your daily calm routine, and later when you work or go out with friends and are all energetic and wide awake. The same analogy applies for your self, your Whole Being including the physical and metaphysical self of you. There are three main stages of awakening to your real Self.

Caterpillar phase - An itch/nudge for change. The pain of staying the same triggers us to search for answers.

Cocoon phase - Inspiration and realization. You discover the power of solitude which is where you internalize new ideas and realizations. You rediscover your true self.

Butterfly phase - explorations and shadow work. You experience what used to be familiar to you but from a completely new way of seeing/realizing things. What was unknown before and hidden, is no more. It comes to light. Shadow dissipates in the presence of the Light.

Start living differently from the masses, when you do that, you will see that it will make a lot of people uncomfortable because they are used to a one size fit all/hive mentality. When you stop playing the game of fear and drama like you were conditioned to, you make others uncomfortable and aware of their limitations. When you function/operate in authentic/love frequency, they don't even know how to approach you because their thinking is very limited. When someone lives in constant fear, anxiety and worry they operate with their reptilian brain, the lower fight or flight part of the brain.

Therefore, not enough oxygen goes in the front of their brain where consciousness/logic is located. This means that they have become less intelligent. You have outgrown their energy; they operate in a low vibrational field. When you become different, people don't know where to fit you.

No matter how much they try they won't be able to. It's like fitting a square into a circle. Your existence, your new you transcends their preconceived ideas. Their expectations of you won't be met anymore because you don't have the same hive mind mentality. The fact that you are reading this book means that you are escaping or have already escaped the hive mind/ conditioned state of mind/lifestyle. Embrace your growth, look for new horizons, new people that vibrate on the same frequency as you and you will see that the sky's the limit.

Do not look down on them though, you were at one point at their level. We all are brothers and sisters. It's that everyone is at a different level in their soul's journey. For some people, the big progress will be made within one lifetime/reincarnation and for others it might take many lifetimes. You are not obligated at all to keep being friends with those that drag you down.

You have your own path to follow just like everyone is on their own path of the journey. Many people remain friends or partners because they think that they will be alone if they lose each other (there are exceptions such as when there are children in the middle). Trust me, there are many new friends that you can meet. I speak from personal experience. As soon as I let go of what was holding me back, which were some friends, co-workers and family members, the path to reach the stars opened.

Do not fall for the victim mentality, everyone beside yourself is on their own life path at their own rate. Do not fall prey to circumstances. Feed your Soul not your Ego.

Lower self
I am a victim of circumstances
There is never enough
I am alive temporary, that is
scary
I am a machine made of 1's & 0's
I'm in competition with the
world
It's complicated

Higher self
I create my own reality
I live in abundance
I am alive temporarily and that is great.
I am an artist made of infinite energy
I am in harmony with the world

I AM happy

Look at the huge different mindset at the above list. Top equals death, and bottom equals **LIFE**. The choice is clear. Your existence is meaningful. Respect and bow to the creator that gave you LIFE. In my humbled opinion, I think we are the most sophisticated beings ever created, at least on a physical level.

GRATEFULNESS - THE REMEDY OF LACK. FOOD FOR YOUR SOUL

Even if you don't have what you would like to be grateful for (just being alive is already a big thing to be grateful for), you must believe and write it as if you already have it. If you believe that you have it, then by the law of attraction, the universe must conspire for you to have it. If you complain that you don't have something, you are sending the energy of lack of abundance and by the law of attraction it's what you will attract, what you think/believe.

Write things you are grateful for every day at the beginning of the day, combining exercise, deep breathing, and will/passion to be strong and healthy, and you will see how your days, weeks, months, and years will turn out to be. We manifest our thoughts. I was on an artistic block for months. I had not drawn/painted or continued writing this book.

It can happen to anyone. I was talking with my good friend Tuyen, a friend of mine that I never met in real life (not that it matters much) about books. It reinforced my will to go back and keep writing this book and eventually it manifested physically. The more you talk about something, the more chance that it will manifest physically. This doesn't mean that if you talk nonstop about a spaceship and it will just materialize in front of you, that's not how it works. There are many different layers of manifestations.

> For individual manifestations, individual concentration of energy is required. For other kinds of manifestations, then collective concentration of energy is required.

So be mindful of your thoughts. Aim for thoughtless experience. Go with the flow and not against it. Desiring to be thoughtless is a desire in itself. Be patient, determined and with practice you will manage to align energetically both the physical (body) and metaphysical (soul) part of you. Be grateful for everything you have.

Do not focus on what you think you don't have. Lack of abundance is an illusion. Everything is available, but you must vibrate in the frequency of abundance which is the same frequency as gratitude.

REINCARNATION

"How many thoughts can a person entertain within one lifetime? Is it fathomable to think that a human being can fulfil every wish within the 70 or 80 years of their life? Would it not make more sense to have numerous lifetimes by which to carry out every desire? This is what many traditions call reincarnations." -The Ancient Ones

Reincarnation is the truth, and here's why: Everything in the universe is made of atoms. An atom itself is made up of three tiny kinds of particles called subatomic particles: protons, neutrons, and electrons. However, quantum physics says that as you go deeper and deeper into an atom to see what's there, you'll find that there is nothing, it is just energy waves.

An atom is basically an invisible forcefield, a kind of miniature tornado, which emits waves of electricity. So, everything in the universe is made up of atoms, and atoms are made up of energy. Your physical body, the human spirit/soul, the air you breathe, your life essence, and everything that makes you "YOU," is made up of energy. Energy cannot be created or destroyed. The total amount of energy in existence has always been the same.

The form that energy takes, however, is constantly changing. This includes the energy that makes up the human soul. It cannot be destroyed. It only changes form. The law of conservation of energy, also known as the first law of thermodynamics, states that the energy of a closed system must remain constant—it can neither increase nor decrease without interference from outside.

This realm (the universe as we know it) is in fact a closed system, (thanks to the firmament) which means nothing enters this realm and nothing leaves this realm... The energy that exists here has always been here. The energy that makes you "YOU" has been here within this realm since the dawn of Creation. We were witness to it all, we just don't remember.

YOU ARE ENERGY
YOU ARE ETERNAL

You cannot be destroyed, no matter what any man-made written doctrine claims.

When your physical body dies, your soul remains alive and well right here in this realm. It doesn't go to "heaven" or "hell" because based on the etymology of those words, they don't exist as physical places/geographical locations. We just transfer our consciousness to a new body when we die.

There's no way this isn't true if the laws of nature and the laws of thermodynamics are accurate and true. This is also proof that "God" is just energy. Just consciousness. Which explains how we, made up of atoms of energy waves, are supposedly **"created in the image of God."**

WE ARE ETERNAL SOULS, WANDERING AROUND THE COSMOS (WITHING MANY DIFFERENT DIMENSIONS) THROUGHOUT INFINITE LIFETIMES, SO THAT WE EXPAND EVEN FURTHER OUR KNOWLEDGE AND INNERSTANDING OF THE UNIVERSE.

Be grateful for everything you have. You will meet the same people over and over but dressed in a different flesh costume. Actors dressed differently throughout all the lifetimes.

PART FOUR

MAGIC

PILLS

**THE SEEN AND THE UNSEEN
ARE ONE AND THE SAME**

What is Magic?

Is it fake or is it **REAL**
You must think and **FEEL**
And what seems like impossibility
it is true and very **REAL**

You body Is **Magic**
your Mind and you **SOUL**
When you align them together
You will reach the **GOAL**

The goal is to lose your **MIND**
and open your **HEART**
To be grateful, empathetic and **KIND**
Your biological body, is pure Universal **ART**
 You are *MAGIC*

                    -Saimir Kercanaj

Chapter **ONE**

MAGICAL HEALTHY PILLS
THAT YOU POSSESS

Below there is a super daily routine that I practice daily which includes the so-called magic pills that you already possess. Depending on your availability and motivations you can add more or subtract some. But I strongly advise doing all these as they all are fundamental for a healthy **BODY, MIND** and **SOUL**. Read the explanation of each one and be the judge of it.

Depending on the level that you may be because you may not innerstand any explanation or not believing it does not make it untrue or useless. You must put in the effort, there is no external magic pill. **YOU** are the **MAGIC**. Shine it out. Light the candle that you possess within. If you don't take time for your wellness, rest assured that you will be forced to take time for your illness.

Stretching
Drinking
Defecating
Urine Therapy (wait, what?
Brushing your teeth
Tongue scraping
Breathing Exercises
Warm up/Exercises
Raw Fruit/Vegetables
Barefoot Walking
Read A Book
Walk/Jog/Run
Fasting
Meditating
Observational and Thoughtless

Perform this routine everyday as if the doctor gave you only a few weeks or months to live. If the doctor told you that you do have only a short time to live in this beautiful PLANEt (the italic word is not a typo;), would you do the impossible to save yourself? Of course, you would, because you love your life, and you deserve to be and live a healthy lifestyle.

If you do this super healthy routine as if you have only a few weeks or months to live, besides the actual physical dividend that you will achieve, you also strengthen the will and the purpose in life. You will elongate the telomeres, which means elongating life. Glossary page will have the explanation of telomeres.

Now we're going to look in detail throughout this list, so you have an innerstanding of how they work and how to incorporate them in your daily life. It is not only important of HOW to do something but it's also important to know/innerstand the WHY. If I say that it's necessary to stretch as soon as you open your eyes before getting up, you might say "ok, I guess it's good to stretch".

But you most likely will not do it. But if I explain to you the important reason, then you will be shocked or wowed at how crucial stretch before lifting your body off the bed is. And I'm sure you will follow the simple super important advice for the simple fact that you decided to get this book and the fact that you made it this far shows that you indeed care about your temple (body). By taking care of your body, you also plant the seed of success for others. You become the blueprint of happiness. You become an example of vitality.

You are planting seeds not only for you but for generations to come. If there were no freedom fighters or nutritionists/homeopathic human beings in previous generations, then we wouldn't be where we are. This book and many others are a testament that health information has survived thanks to those that have fought hard for us. We must also fight hard at disseminating information for the next generations.

FIRST SEED OF THE DAY

<u>FIRST SEED OF THE DAY</u>

Stretching

Before getting up, as soon as you open your eyes after you wake up in this dream called life, you MUST stretch your body. Well, depending on if your eyes are open, you may still stay in bed for a few min, but you **must stretch before you raise up your body from the bed**. Start by wiggling your toes, ankles, knees, fingers, wrists and breathe deeply a few times with your diaphragm for a couple of minutes. When you read that you must breathe with the diaphragm, it also means with the chest also.

Remember? Fill up your belly until full, keep breathing with your chest until it is full of air and only then exhale completely before having to inhale again. All this to be done while you are lying down. (The complete breathing of diaphragm/chest should be done 24/7 , it is how it must be to be super healthy).

Stretching before getting up is super important because **all night 40-50% of your blood is concentrated in your liver and pancreas for purification**. If you get up suddenly without stretching, your heart must work hard against gravity and to distribute the blood everywhere in your body so it can deliver oxygen while the body is in movement. The damage that the heart receives is accumulative. Even if you are young with no heart problems, your heart gets damaged regardless.

And if you are not young then definitely you must do the warming up and make sure the body has adequate blood/oxygen. Before you start up the car, the oils and all other fluids are settled all night or all day if the car was parked for a few hours. You must let the car run for a few minutes before taking off. The same with your body.

Statistically most heart attacks happen in the morning for the reason (40-50% of the blood being in the liver and pancreas) I mentioned previously. If you nap let's say for 2 or 3 hours, you must again stretch because it applies the same as when you wake up after the night sleep. I'm refraining from using the word morning as the true meaning is mourning. But let's move on from the meaning of it, that's another subject that has to do with the manipulation of the mind. So, let's move on...

DRINKING

After you get up, the first thing you should do is to drink water as your body has been many hours with only whatever amount you drank the day/night before. You have seen that usually the first urine of the day is darker than during the day where it is pale white or yellowish. Air and water are the 2 main things that your body always needs to operate. Try to open the window of your room so clean fresh air gets in.

Have one medium or large glass of warm water with honey and lemon or lime or apple cider vinegar.

One medium glass of water with chia seeds and cucumber slices.

One glass of fruit smoothie. These three glasses of water to be drank within 30min after you get off the bed. Once or twice a week when you take a bath, add half a cup of baking soda.

The baking soda must be food grade and aluminum free. Add a handful of Epsom salt, a few (5-10) drops of lavender essential oil, or any other flavor but make sure it is food grade as your skin is also an organ.

Anything that goes on your skin will go inside of you. This kind of bath will soften rough, dry skin, and exfoliate dead skin cells. It will reduce soreness and pain. This ingredient combo will draw out toxins, it will lower stress related hormones, and balance your body's PH levels.

Be soft and smooth like water
Reach high and be strong like a mountain
Flow with passion and be alive like a river
Be calm and patient like a lake
Feed your temple with oxygen
Fill your mind with clarity
Fill your soul with purpose
Fill the world with Love
Spread around you Light
Never give up the fight
Water is your friend
Water is your savior
Water loves you and you can love it back

Get busy by peeing all day, that way you won't have time for other people's dramas.

EXIT NUMBER TWO

If you eat healthy then you should be able to defecate after one hour you ate a meal. You must squat, the way the intestines are placed by squatting they get massaged and straightened out for easy excretion. Squatters do it better. Look at nature and you will see that all animals squat to defecate. Our closest ancestors, the primates, squat with their knees drawn up to their chest.

By squatting, it opens anal area more directly. While squatting, stretch arms up above head so the transverse colon will empty easier. Even today many human beings still defecate in this natural manner, especially in the Middle East, Africa, and Asia. The sit-down toilets may save your legs the effort required to squat properly, but it is a device that tortures your bowels and the problems it causes are not worth the effort saved.

Squatting while using the toilet is the most natural way for the colon. When you pinch the intestines, you make it harder on the digestive system. So, you must lift your feet close to the chest. If you are not handy to build a squatting wooden device, then using a step stool to squat is more than fine. Your colon (large intestine) is as long as you are tall.

The diameter of your colon is equal to that of your wrist. For every foot of colon, you can store roughly 5-10lb (2-4 kg) of feces. A healthy person should have 2-3 bowel movements every day, unless you are fasting, which in that case you might have one bowel movement or none, depending on whether you are water, juice or smoothie fasting.

The colon reabsorbs fluids 8-10 times every 30 minutes. The colon has referral areas that are similar to the reflexology points on your hands and feet. To the degree your colon is clean, is to the degree your bloodstream is clean. Your colon has without a doubt a few pounds/kg of putrefied filthy food/mucus/pus etc. One of the best ways to clean it up is by fasting.

When a body needs to heal, you don't add more to the system, regardless of eating healthy or not. For the fact that all the energy of your body must be used to purify your system instead of digesting more foods that you add to eat. There is only one 100% for the whole body. For example: If 80% of the energy is used to digest the food and its process from the moment you eat to the moment you have to defecate, there is only 20& left to take care of all other organs, purifying your blood etc. What can 20% do? SO, it is more efficient to not eat, instead of fasting.

That way the system has all the available 100% to purify you from head to toes. The body must be nourished with deep correct breathing, raw food, purified water, healthy thinking, meditation and so on so it can heal itself. Squatting must be an everyday habit. If your colon is clogged (which it is) with filth, pus, mucus, and other poison residues, it doesn't matter how healthy you eat.

You don't just add new oil on top of the old oil in your car. First you empty the old oil before replacing it with new one. Mixing both good and bad oils together, it will only become muddy, unhealthy. First thing in the morning while you do the warmup exercises before you even get up, rub your hands briskly for a few seconds, put one hand on top of the other and massage/rub in circles the abdomen. This way you are massaging the bowel/large intestine and will help it get ready for excretion later on when you get to the bathroom.

A good method for alleviating chronic constipation is to use your fingertips and gently massage the soft region between the anus and the tip of the spinal column (coccyx). It will directly stimulate the colon and help sluggish bowels to evacuate more thoroughly. In addition, also practice the anal sphincter exercise rhythmically by contracting and relaxing the sphincter several times a day.

This exercise stimulates glands in the anus to secrete natural lubrication, which greatly facilitates movement of dry stools. Also, stale blood will be flushed from the anal sphincter, thereby preventing formation of hemorrhoids. A clean unobstructed colon is one of the most important prerequisites on the road to health and longevity.
The anal exercise to be exercise daily regardless of if you have chronic constipation or not. PLEASE SQUAT

Your amazingly created biologically body needs nothing external to heal itself. You can take all the herbs, vitamins, and supplements you want, and they would be no way near to what urine can do for you. Your urine has stem cells, hormones, vital salts, minerals, and many other beneficial elements which make it the best remedy for any disease that the body has, but you must also be living a decent lifestyle. The more polluted your body is, the more it will take you to notice differences in your well-being.

Urine Therapy is Nature's own Perfect Medicine

"For almost the entire course of the 20th century, unknown to the public, doctors and medical researchers have been proving in both laboratory and clinical testing that our own urine is an enormous source of vital nutrients, vitamins, hormones, enzymes and critical antibodies that cannot be duplicated or derived from any other source. They use urine for healing cancer, heart disease, allergies, auto-immune diseases, diabetes, asthma, infertility, infections, wounds and on and on -- yet we're taught that urine is a toxic waste product. This discrepancy between the medical truth and the public information regarding urine is ludicrous and, as the news releases you've just read demonstrate, can mean the difference between life and death to you and to your loved ones."

IS IT GOLD?

Urine is filtered blood plasma, medically referred to as *"plasma ultrafiltrate."* Before appreciating urine and its benefits, you must unlearn the misinformation that you were taught to believe about what it is. Urine is not a dirty substance excreted by your body. It is a by-product of blood filtration, and not waste filtration. Urine is a purified blood derivative, made by the kidneys, whose main function is not excretion, but regulation of all the elements and their concentrations in the blood.

Nutrient-filled blood passes through the liver where toxins are removed to be excreted as solid waste. This purified clean blood undergoes a filtering process in the kidneys, where excess water, salts, vitamins, enzymes, minerals, urea, antibodies, uric acid, and other elements that are not usable at the time by the body, are collected in the form of a purified, sterile, watery solution which is called "urine." So, you see that your urine is very rich and very beneficial for you. Oh, now that I recalled something.

When you consume coffee, or soft drinks which are neurotoxins many of the minerals, enzymes, antibodies etc are expelled unnecessarily (which your body really needs). Which means that it is very important to drink your urine especially when the minerals, enzymes etc are expelled unnecessarily in the case of having consumed coffee or soft drink prior.

Any neurotoxic substance is a foreign organism for your body, so your body will use its water to expel it. Since you now know what is in your urine, wouldn't it make sense to not consume neurotoxin products (sugar is the worst legal drug neurotoxin) and to consume urine? Probably I don't have to say it but I'm going to say it anyway, because you never know, I've seen people that have said and done the unthinkable.

What I'm trying to say is that you must consume your own urine and not that of your neighbour. Yes, yes, I can hear your thoughts that it's common sense, but you would be surprised that common sense is not so common.

One of the most powerful healings comes from **URINE FASTING**. Urine fast is essentially a water fast where you also consume everything you pass. Urine fasting/therapy is very effective because fasting puts the body in a healing state, by leaving all its energy for healing instead for digesting solid food. On top of consuming raw fruit/veggies, exercising urine fasting is like putting your healing process on steroids (natural steroids).

Urine fasting is very, very powerful, but it will not do its job fully or in a short time of practicing it when your body is clogged with junk food, junk thoughts, junk liquids, junk feelings (actions/inactions as a reaction to unhealed self/emotions). Urine will help you but by itself will have to work against a mountain of previously mentioned junks. SO, it is very advisable that you also exercise, eat healthy and fast (check fasting chapter in later pages.) Even if you are fully convinced (which you will eventually, depending on how serious you are about your health), that urine therapy is indeed very beneficial, you can't think that: "Ok, I will keep consuming crap, so urine therapy will make up for it". It doesn't work like that.

Either you are all in or out. Just as I mentioned the analogy of changing the oil of your car. You don't just add the good oil or part of it in the dirty oil that needs to be changed and expect to fix the problem. Urine will keep your body functioning better. Without addressing your diet/lifestyle, urine benefits are limited. Is like consuming fast food, processed food, ice-cream, soft drink, meat and at the end of the day you eat a big bowl of vegetable salad. What is that going to do?

-Nothing, as the junk food takes priority for digestion, while the good food that can digest fast gets fermented on top of the acidic/cancerous food that you had. **Urine Therapy is the magic pill when combined with a fast and/ or clean diet**. Your lifestyle/diet is what will sustain your good health. John Armstrong, the author of 'The water of LIFE' cured thousands of people with urine therapy.

Urine therapy is a wonderful cure. It will heal many ailments even if you don't change your diet, but the real benefits are when they (urine and healthy diet) work synergistically as it will heal the dangerous diseases as without lifestyle change will only heal minor diseases (minor disease can turn into major).

When you research "urine therapy", the main search engines most likely will say that no scientific evidence exists or any other exclamation as to dismiss the benefits of urine therapy. Hmm, who decides what is true and what is not?

Have in mind that most scientific so-called research is done in a controlled environment by the same $cientists that have personal gains. Many studies' results are to the satisfaction of those that gain from the results. I don't know your age, but back in time when we got hurt, let's say the leg, we would pee on the wound to disinfect it.

Do we need $cience to tell us if its ok to do it or not? Unfortunately, as a society we are conditioned to beLIEve $cience and doctors (drug dealers). And as a result, we pay for it by giving our power away to corporations that only profit is their main concern. Urine therapy/consumption may be hard for you or many others to grasp, and that is precisely because of conditioning. We were never taught knowledge about our body.

Once you realize how powerful your body is and how insanely efficiently it is designed, then it will all make sense. **Your body makes its own medicine and self-heals**. Urine consumption has helped reverse even the most degenerated bodies to homeostasis. HOW? Because urine contains information about everything that is wrong with your body. When you ingest urine, the glands that you have in your throat will pick up the information of the urine and will instantly produce antibodies for whatever is wrong with you.

As an important example for an urgent situation: If you get bit by a snake or stung by a bee, drink your urine and the poison should be neutralized from your system.

If you are a degenerate food addict, do not expect urine to fix a mental problem that you have. After urine therapy you have to be feeling better, but if you go back to consuming crap, then the diseases will return. An important thing to keep in mind about your health is:

To keep bladder and sphincter muscles tight and tones, urinate-stop-urinate-stop 4-5 times, twice daily when voiding, especially after the age of 40. This simple exercise works wonders for both men and women. Even if you are below the age of 40 you should still do this. You may be 27 or 35 on paper, but your internal body may be older than that of a 40-year young person.

I refrain from using the word OLD when referring to age. I wrote a whole long chapter about why we age in my book *"I AM THE KEY THAT OPENS ALL DOORS."* Okay, let's get back to the urine subject and wrap the chapter up. If there was an earthquake and you got trapped for many days or if you got trapped in other situations, do you know how you can survive? By drinking your own urine of course.

Depending on which group you belong (1-those that beLIEve religiously the $cience or 2- those that are ready to explore things from a different viewpoint and judge by yourself by using common sense and personally experimenting, instead of blindly beLIEving others instead of being your own scientist by having gained an educated unbiased opinion), you will either disbeLIEve and ridicule this section or you will/might give it a second thought and research it. Fear is the enemy of progress.

Fear breeds ignorance. I broke the chains of ignorance when I finally started practicing urine therapy. You can just start by drinking a small amount. Use the lid of a water bottle as a start for a few days or weeks. Or use a jar or whatever you prefer. The healthier you eat and drink, the better your urine will taste.

Not that you would like to taste it, you have no choice but to taste it when you swallow it (I mentioned to you before, stop thinking dirty:). When you decide to go with this amazing therapy, the first few times keep the urine in the mouth, so you get used to the idea of it, and after a few times then begin to swallow it, in small amounts each time and increase later on. The first few times empty the small amount (from the bottle lid) under your tongue.
As there are no taste buds there, plus the skin is so thin there that it is also beneficial by just keeping it there a few sec as there is the thick blood vein that will instantly absorb elements from your urine.

So much for wrapping up the chapter eh?
On top of drinking it, you can also put it on your skin. While you are in the bathroom (or anywhere else) when you pee on the cup for drinking it, also pee on a cloth so you can rub your face with it and then wash it up. Also, you can rub all your body with it before having shower. I was scoffing and making fun of people meditating, I ended up meditating regularly.

I was making fun of people fasting, I also ended up fasting regularly. I was having fun and was disgusted by people drinking their own urine (magic healing liquid pill) and rubbing their skin with it. I also do this now. I am a different person now. I have clear thoughts, emotions, and feel physically stronger than ever.

I don't expect you to rush and drink your own urine. But please at least consider it. Do some research. First important thing is to innerstand what exactly is urine, when you know what it is then you will know that not only that is not harmful at all, but instead is the healing elixir you already possess, and it is free, and it never runs out. It is available every day.

My face's wrinkles are disappearing from practicing urine therapy and the usual everyday physical exercises, especially the exercise where I rub my hands with each other and then I rub around my eyes, around ears, along the side of the nose and all the face.

By rubbing your hands together, they produce Chee energy (life force energy), so this energy makes the stagnant blood (in the wrinkles) flow. You can easily get rid of all wrinkles. Well except in places where they are required such as: Your nuts (if you have any), your elbows as the skin needs room to stretch for the elbows when you stretch your arms or for your almonds (nuts) when you walk or sit down.

YOU POSSESS LIQUID GOLD WITHIN

I believe now you have some innerstanding about the benefits of urine. Not only by drinking it but also by rubbing your skin with it. I suggest that every morning when you go to the bathroom, on a small cloth (towel) wet it with urine and rub your face with it and then rinse your face with water of course if you are living with other people, or let it dry out if you live by yourself.

After a few min it shouldn't smell. On top of using urine on your face, you should use it also all over your body's skin. When you use it on your body's skin, make sure it is the day that you will have a shower. Again, with a well wet towel go all over your body and hair (the root of it).

After you done the shower you will see how smooth your skin will be if it is not already smooth. Just rub your face and arms softly with your hand, to see how nice and smooth your skin is. You are the factory of the biological healthiest natural pill.

Since the first urine of the day when you wake up is concentrated which means it will smell a bit, and taste weird, I would suggest that get ready a glass of water with honey, or any other juice (healthy one of course) that you can drink after you drink your urine, so you won't have to taste the little weird after taste. I don't do this. I just deal with the taste and the weird smell.

The reason why I don't do it is so I can remain strong and determined. I remember the first times when I tried avocado, I had to spit it out, it tasted so weird. But after a while I got used to the taste, and since then (it's been over 10 years now) I eat an avocado every day. It doesn't mean that you will get used to the urine smell or taste (I think you will get used to it), but by challenging yourself, it will be easier when you try weird things next time.

Remember that it is in the head that notion of "that's disgusting" about the urine because it comes out of your genitals. It's how you perceive things.

You can perceive something to be good/bad or tasty/disgusting based on your conditioning that you have been gone through or based on your independent, critical thinking research and personal experience. Just like meat can taste very good for you, but it is actually rotten corpse. No matter how much research you can do, you still have to put it in practice, by experimenting yourself whatever is that you research.

Depending on how strong minded you are, when you research something, you will tend to believe those articles/books that align with your beLIEfs. Which means you may stay in your comfortable bubble. **You cannot progress by staying in the same place**.

Expand your thinking. In this case is about your health. Why do you consume without a second thought an ice cream, or a chocolate, or any of thousands of fake, artificial unhealthy products? Because you were conditioned by repetition. Repeating something enough times, becomes a new beLIEf. Be always ready and willing to undo any current belief and consider other new ways of thinking and experiencing things in life. Urine is the river of life. Blood is the river of life. Since urine is a purified blood, what does that make urine?

Have you considered it yet?
Or
are you still scoffing at the idea?

Wow, I'm still going, aren't I? I better hurry up so you can start the therapy;)
As we now know that urine is purified blood, then that leaves us with the question: **Why kill ourselves slowly with external poison when we can drink from the fountain of youth?** Are you in or ...in? You already know that you are smart and will do what's best for your health. For this urine therapy (UT) a hardcore decision must be made for the simple fact of mental conditioning we have been through for a long time. We have been conditioned to reject natural creation and accept lab-made poison/chemicals that only destroy human health slowly or faster. Your body is one of CREATOR's labs.

You are the alchemist. One thing to have in mind is that you should aim for a healthy, empowered life and not only longevity. Many sick people have lived longer than healthier ones but because they were on pills, like zombies, while the healthier ones lived their life to the fullest. A reason why some very healthy people live a short life is because they could have achieved LIGHT BODY and they decided to leave our realm at will in their sleep. But this is a topic for a different time. What you should focus on is yourself and now.

Are you out or are you IN?

YOU'RE IN (urine) is the best filtered juice that you can find. No other juice will be as clean and filtered as your urine. I wouldn't even consider the thought of thinking about this therapy years ago. Because I had no innerstanding. I was spending lots of money on healthy food. I thought the food I was buying, was healthy, the perception of it being healthy it's what tricks us.

Do you know what they put on the food? Like pesticides, herbicides, preservatives, and many other artificial crap that are not meant to be processed naturally by our body. So, I started researching and questioning my body's abilities. I ended up eating less, fasting, meditation, sunbathing, barefoot walking, exercising and urine therapy which was the last thing for me to consider.

It's all about perception. If you have been conditioned to think that urine is a waste, then you will not consider it, which you lose as you deny the beauty and importance of your super biological technological body that you are given by the creator. Not your parents as your parents didn't create you, they built you. The creator created the ingredient and the procedure and how everything functions in your body. You didn't come from your parents. You came **FROM** the Creator **THROUGH** your parents.

The choice as always is yours. Either you practice this therapy of free endless supply or spend lots of money and worry about your health by consuming lots of crap that are designed to keep you sick in a degenerative state.

Key Points to remember

1- Make sure you don't miss the first urine of the day
2- Start with a small amount at first
3- When peeing stop, let go, stop, let go until the last drop.
4- Keep urine in mouth for 10 sec before swallowing when starting the therapy. Later on, you can drink a whole glass/jar of it.
5- First few times spit it out until you get used to the taste or no. It is not as bad as you may think.
6- Leave this therapy for last until after you practice all points of PART FOUR if you think it is difficult at first.
7- Don't smell it for a few secs until you swallow the morning batch. During the day, urine shouldn't smell or taste bad.

P. S. Starting with small amount at first means by not sipping it. Whatever amount you decide to drink, drink the whole thing without stopping, so you will taste it only once after you done drinking it instead of many times by sipping it.

YOU ARE THE ALCHEMIST THAT PRODUCE YOUR OWN LIQUID GOLD (MAGIC PILL)

PIT OF HELL IF NOT TAKEN CARE OF

I can't believe that I must write about brushing our teeth, but because we have been conditioned for a long time mentally, emotionally, and physically to use/consume unhealthy products. And as a result, we have a sick, degenerate society. Dental hygiene is an essential part of our day. Besides preventing cavities, brushing your teeth, protects the brain.

Countless research shows that people with poor oral health are predisposed to diseases that can cause memory loss such as Alzheimer's and dementia.

Animal studies show that rats with missing teeth had worse memory loss than those who had full sets of teeth. This is because memory is formed by sensory impulses produced by movement in the jaw. The memory-forming part of the brain is called hippocampus. When you chew, the hippocampus becomes activated by the motions of your teeth and jaw. Which means that the less healthy dental hygiene (in this case missing teeth), the fewer impulses are sent to the hippocampus and the fewer memories we hold.

When your gums and teeth feel good, you feel good. Research shows (don't ask me for sources, you have the same technology as me for research) a clear link between gum disease and mood conditions like anxiety, stress, and depression. What causes your teeth and gum disease? Do I have to answer this? Ok, I will: Food and drinks and improper breathing. **Oral health is one of the key points to brain health.**

Why risk when just a few minutes a day of your time can save your health?

Most of us are lazy, especially if we are in bed, on our phone, we may feel drowsy and would rather fall asleep than getting up and brushing our teeth. It is a minor inconvenience. Losing a tooth to an infection can be much riskier than people realize. There can be plenty of complications, some can even be deadly. Having infected teeth, you may even get cancer or hepatitis. The teeth are connected with the rest of the body. Which means that the bacteria that caused the infection, can move anywhere, even in your brain.

Do you realize how serious it is to not brush your teeth and scrape your tongue? DO NOT use a toothpaste with fluoride in it. Fluoride is not the only poison in toothpastes. So, don't get deceived by the wording fluoride free on toothpastes you buy. It's a marketing term.

The question shouldn't be what is free of but what else does it have inside. It can be free of 3-4 poison chemicals, but it may have 7-8 other lab-made junk ones. So, the best solution is to make your own toothpaste with coconut oil and baking soda (food grade-aluminum free one).

Respect and follow this rule and your health will improve:

Never use a product externally that you wouldn't ingest internally. Coconut oil and baking soda are 100% safe to ingest, so, wouldn't it make sense to brush your teeth with it?

Because you don't ingest something, it doesn't mean that it doesn't go into the bloodstream. The bottom of your mouth, below the tongue that area is covered with a super thin skin layer, where you can easily see the blood vein. So, as you can see, any bacteria or chemicals (from store bought toothpastes) can easily go into your bloodstream even if you don't ingest it.

Once a week put the toothbrush for half an hour in a small glass of water with lemon or lime to destroy the bacteria that get accumulated on the toothbrush.

SCRAPE YOUR TONGUE AND TASTE
THE BEAUTY OF FOOD

Tongue scraping must be as important a routine as brushing your teeth. Before you brush your teeth, scrape your tongue with a tongue scraper plastic or metal or if you don't feel like buying one you can use a tablespoon. With the side of the spoon, starting from the middle of the tongue while gradually starting from farther back as you get used to scraping. This will prevent gaggling. Scrape gently to not break the skin or alter the taste buds.

After scraping (let's use the spoon as a reference) you will see and be shocked at what filth the spoon will catch. Don't scrape from the tip of your tongue backwards, if you do that then the bacteria will end up at the back of your tongue and you don't want to swallow it. After finishing with scraping, wash the scraper or the spoon with soap and make sure you leave it in a dry area.

Do it a few times one after another before brushing your teeth. Also, during the day if you remember, which you should. It's very important that you have a healthy mouth. A mouth full of bacteria will affect your teeth, brain, heart, and the rest of your body. With every consumption of food that you eat, comes debris that just sticks on your tongue and sometimes these are difficult to remove without a tongue scraper.

The debris tends to build up on your tongue if they are not removed to a point where they harbor bacteria over time. These bacteria are the leading cause of bad breath and plaque which negatively impact your oral health. When you scrape your tongue on a regular basis, your taste buds are improved and you can enjoy your food with the ability to distinguish between sensations such as: sour, salty, bitter, and sweet.

With all the artificial flavored food that people consume, the taste buds are confused, and their sensory ability diminished. When your tongue is clean, foods with artificial flavours that you thought were sweet, now will seem overly sweet.

That's why people consuming unhealthy food and drinks want more and more of the same as they cannot distinguish real natural taste from artificial. Also, they build muscle memory where they associate crappy food with good food, but it is a deception that they pay with their health. Tongue scraping balances the mouth and gut microbiome.

CONTRAINDICATIONS:
DO not scrape hard to the point that it could lead to cutting, or bleeding as these open wounds could easily harbor bacteria leading to infection.

Inducing vomit will affect your digestive system while compromising your teeth as you regurgitate acids which could harm your teeth eventually.

Gag reflex stimulation can lead to vomiting so that's why it is advisable to start first in the middle of the tongue and then gradually start scraping further back.

Using an uneven or short tool can lead to accidental cuts. To prevent that, inspect regularly whichever tool you are using to scrape your tongue.

Chapter **TWO**

BREATHING EXERCISES

Breathing exercises must be practiced as if your life depends on it. There are different breathing exercises. They all have different benefits. Some (inhalation) enhance and assimilate the circulation and assimilation of oxygen and Chee, while others (exhalation) focus on rapid expulsion of toxins from the lungs and bloodstream, while some others stimulate and sedate the system. If you have never practiced deep abdominal breathing, should first familiarize yourself with the diaphragm by performing the following exercise:

Lie flat on your back on a solid surface (on the carpet), lawn, floor, or any other hard surface, but not a mattress or any other soft places. Relax your body with your legs slightly opened, arms down by your side, and neck comfortably stretched. Place the palm on your abdomen just below the navel and place the other palm against your rib cage. Thoroughly empty your lungs, start inhaling slowly through your nose, directing the airstream down to the bottom of your lungs. You should feel your lower abdomen swell up as you inhale. When the abdomen stops swelling, continue inhalation and feel the rib cage expand as the mid lungs fill with air.

Retain the breath for a few seconds, then begin a long, slow, controlled exhalation through the nose. You will feel the rib cage shrink first, followed by the contraction of the lower abdomen. This is the sensation that you should feel. Next, place a big heavy book over your lower abdomen and repeat the exercise with the hands down by your sides, raising and lowering the weight with expansions and contractions of the abdominal wall.

After you practice for 1-2 weeks these basic exercises which you should have a firm grasp of how diaphragm and abdominal wall function during deep breathing, begin doing the exercises below:

Bhastrika or Bellow Breaths

Bellow breath is a simple form of Pranayama (or breathing exercise). One of the easier forms of Pranayama to practice, Bellow Breath is popular for its naturally energizing benefits. This breathing technique will purify your lungs and bloodstream of toxins, it will also help clear your mind and give you a natural and immediate boost of energy, so it's perfect to practice any time you need an immediate lift of energy.

This exercise involves breathing forcefully in and out as if you were pumping the bellows of a blacksmith's fire - hence the name Bellow Breaths. Practice this exercise during long-life exercises, at the beginning of deep breathing exercises and whenever your breathing and circulation feel stagnant.

Technique: Make sure you have your tongue firmly against palate and keep it there throughout the exercise. Find a comfortable seat. Sitting tall with your shoulders relaxed and away from the ears, rest your left hand on your leg and right hand on your belly. Note: You can keep both hands on your laps if you wish.

-Take a cleansing breath in through the nose and out through the nose. In cold, dry weathers use the nostrils only; if air is warm and moist, mouth exhalation is preferable. The first round will begin on an inhale.

-Rapidly inhale and exhale through the nose completely and forcibly. Use the diaphragm to pump the movement

-One inhale and exhale equals one round of breath.

-Start with ten rounds of breath and do more or less depending on how intense it feels in your body. - After ten rounds of breath, follow the final expulsion by the deepest possible inhalation.

-Hold that deep breath in as long as you can, comfortably.

-Very slowly release the breath with the deepest possible exhalation.

-The end of this exhalation completes one round of breath.

-Rest a bit (20-30sec) after one round is over by taking a few normal breaths.

-Repeat for three rounds. This exercise clears your mind and the system of the body including the immune system. Performing a few rounds throughout the day can help increase your digestive power and boost metabolism. Despite this relaxation, the sympathetic nervous system is briefly stimulated during practice, which means you may experience heart rate increase and feel your body warm up. After practicing this Pranayama (breathing exercise), the body settles into a parasympathetic system a.k.a. "Rest and digest" mode. Which means that blood pressure and heart rate usually drop to or below the resting rate, and the autonomic nervous system comes back into balance.

DO NOT practice Bellow Breath exercise if you are pregnant, have uncontrolled hypertension, epilepsy, seizures, or panic disorder.

Due to the pumping action of the breath, you should avoid practicing Bellow Breath on a full stomach, wait at least two hours after eating. Since this kind of exercise is an energizing practice, avoid practicing it close to bedtime, as it may also kickstart your mind and you may have difficulties falling asleep.

Benefits: After a few minutes of practicing Bellows Breath, you can feel oxygen flowing into every cell in the body and peacefulness in both body and mind. This exercise is a wonderful way to begin meditation or for an energy boost at any point throughout the day. The Bellows refreshes the brain by irrigating it with oxygen-rich blood. Note how lucid you feel after the Bellows Breath exercise. Try it when you feel physically exhausted, mentally muddled, or emotionally upset.

You'll be surprised at how quickly it restores equilibrium and boosts energy levels. This is an ancient practice that has the ability to change your life and increase your prana (life force energy). Everyone is different so you may take it slower or reduce the number of rounds. You will know what feels comfortable for you. It is better if you practice this or any other exercise as much as you can outside where there is clean fresh air, and if you can't, then open the window so fresh air flows in.

Fractional breathing

Fractional Breathing is a good exercise for beginners to use in developing breath retention. Each breath is inhaled or exhaled incrementally, with mini retentions between segments.

Posture: Sitting or standing is best, but you can also employ the technique while lying or walking.

Technique: To perform fractional inhalation, begin a deep abdominal inhalation, but stop when your lungs are only ¼ to ⅓ full. Apply the anal lock (by contracting the muscle as if you are holding your pee), sink the breath down and retain briefly. Then release the anal lock, but instead of exhaling, continue the inhalation for another ¼ to ⅓ increment, pause, lock up, retain, release lock, and continue in this manner until lungs are full then do a long, complete uninterrupted exhalation.

For fractional exhalation, reverse the process. Take a complete uninterrupted inhalation, lock, and retain briefly, then exhale about ¼ to ⅓ of the breath, stop, lock, and retain, then exhale another increment until lungs are empty. After 2 or 3 fractional breaths, relax the breathing apparatus with a few Bellow breaths, then do one or two more rounds. **Never** practice both fractional inhalation and exhalation on the same breath. Fractional inhalation stimulates the system and should be practiced in the morning, or whenever you need a boost. Fractional exhalation is tranquilizing and should be used at night or whenever you need to calm down.

Benefits: It quickly accustoms the novice to the techniques and sensation of breath retention and the Anal Lock. The shift in pressure and locks promote circulation of blood and energy and stimulate cellular respiration, which causes body heat and benefits metabolism.

<u>Pound upper chest</u>

Most people's lungs are not fully functional from irregular breathing. Some areas of the lungs are unused, the pathways can become narrowed or even closed.

Technique: While standing, take a deep, full diaphragmatic breath and lift your chin up slightly. Once you have taken in the full breath, hold it in and stand still. Then raise your bent arms chest high and with closed fists gently pound your upper chest area (while still holding your breath), in gorilla style. Also pound your rib areas and the lower lung region. Do this for as long as you feel comfortable holding your breath. As you exhale, knees relaxed, bend head down below heart and exhale as much old air as possible from the lungs. Repeat this exercise 3-4 times.

Benefits: This breathing exercise can help rejuvenate the lungs by opening up the passageways to the lungs' neglected areas. With a full breath swelling your lungs, this gentle pounding (patting) exercise opens up the passageways that haven't carried air for a long time. The more passageways you have available to move air through your lungs and into your blood, the more energy and vitality and the better health and fitness you will experience.

<u>Posture breathing</u>

This activity is designed to correct bad posture habits, which are among the greatest impediments to proper breathing. Practice this activity several times a day at home or at work or anywhere. It should bring relief to your tired shoulders, spine, and eyes, making you more alert and energized.

Technique: While sitting relaxed in the chair, let your chin rest on your upper chest as you slowly lean forward, slowly exhaling. With eyes closed, continue leaning until hands and elbows rest comfortably on your upper legs. After slowly exhaling in this position, sit upright quickly while sniffing in a full breath of fresh air through the nose. As you do this, let your eyes open wide and then hold your full breath for ten seconds. If it's too much then begin by 5 seconds and increase when you can. After holding the inhaled breath, slowly release air through the mouth. Then close your eyes, lean forward and then repeat the exercise a couple more times.

Benefits: This exercise corrects body posture. Especially the spine and neck. It is very efficient in making the blood and oxygen flow freely to the brain and the heart doesn't have to work as hard. It is already a big effort for the heart to pump blood against gravity to the brain. Put a sticky note everywhere as a reminder to practice deep diaphragmatic breathing and other exercises. Well, some exercises can be done only when home, or anywhere that doesn't require you to bike, drive, walk etc.

Chapter THREE

WARM UP, STRETCH, LONG LIFE

W hen you innerstand how your body works and how important it is to exercise for your overall health, you would never not want to take care of it. Read any exercise until the end before you perform it as some of them have contraindications. If you have any health problems including back pain, neck pain etc do not perform certain exercises that stretches those areas that you already have pain. It is common sense.

Allow 15-20 seconds between each exercise so you can expel the carbon dioxide and inhale a full amount of fresh air.

Burn bay leaves to relieve anxiety, open the respiratory system except for people that already have respiratory problems which in that case only fresh air accompanied with deep breathing is the best thing. Bay leaves' smoke/ smell increases mindfulness by relaxing the mind. Another herb I suggest you burn is sage (my favorite). I suggest you burn real herbs.

Be careful and do proper research when you buy incense online or offline as there are many fake ones that not only won't do anything good for your health, but they can also harm you. Many are made of plastic or other chemical materials which they just add sage (or other flavours) fake flavours/chemicals. Just like in many fruit juices that you buy at the grocery (supermarket) store have lab made flavours so that the product smells and tastes like the real fruit. Although whoever has clean functioning taste buds in the mouth can tell if the product is healthy or if it has chemicals added.

Deep diaphragmatic breathing by focusing totally on your breath, it shuts up the chattering monkey, that part of the brain that wants to take over you every single moment of your life.

EXERCISES

These exercises may remind you of school (indoctrination facility), but these are about your personal health and not about getting a job and being a productive member of society - Did you detect the sarcasm? The only way to truly be productive for society is to 1st unlock the powers you possess within and shine the light around you so others may open their eyes to their own power.

Fasting #1 remedy about anything.
Fasting
Raw fruit/veggie/nuts/herbs
Deep breathing exercises (with the diaphragm)
Sunbathe
Sun gaze
Meditation
Walk barefoot on grass/soil
Liquid Gold Therapy-Urine Therapy (UT) – The **MAGIC Pill**
Practice solitude (away from people so you can hear your own inner voice and not the opinion of others)

Do this daily, be determined, discipline about it and no disease can touch you. Perform the routine/list as if the doctor gave you only a few months to live.

WARMING UP - Exercises

Before any activity it is especially important that you warm your body. Just like a car needs to be warmed up first. Warming up heats your biological motor, gets your oils (water, blood) moving which in turns tunes the moving parts. This warmup set requires 3-5 minutes to perform and may be practiced as an exercise any time of the day besides every morning, which is a requirement necessary to start the day, so you won't be stiff. Exercises should be performed daily to relax any cramped, fatigued body parts, stimulating the circulation of blood and energy and to diminish the chances of pulling a muscle.

Overhead arm reach

Technique: Stand up with your feet hip-width apart. Swing your left arm overhead to your right side. Whilst swinging your arm left, twist your torso, and pivot your opposite foot inward. Then return back to the original position and repeat the same thing on the opposite side with your other arm.

Benefits: The overhead arm reach is the best exercise to kickstart energy and muscle warmth. An all-over body warm up is ideal for every type of exercise. Arm reach exercise fires up all areas of your body and not just your arms. Repeat this 5 or so times before moving onto the next exercise.

Spine and torso twist

Stand upright when performing this exercise. This is one of the best beneficial physical warm-up exercises. It's best to practice it several times daily as a preventive measure against congestion in the digestive tract, misalignment of spinal vertebrae and stiffness in the hips.

Technique: Standing upright, keep feet a few inches (one inch=2.5cm) apart, relax your shoulders, and arms. Use only your thighs for torque, twist the trunk and torso slowly right and left. Gently increase the torque and extend the twist, letting your arms flail out loosely by the sides. Shoulders, elbows, wrists should be totally loose and arm muscles relaxed throughout the whole exercise.
drawing

SPINE AND TORSO
TWIST

Benefits: If you hear a crackling sound along your spine during the first few twists, it means that your vertebrae are realigning themselves into proper positions. The torso twists, stabilizes the spine and allows movement by coordinating with the pelvis muscles. These muscles work together to flex, extend, bend, and rotate.

Contraindication:
Performing torso rotation exercises while seated can result in spine and back pain. The risk to your lower back can be avoided by performing the exercise ONLY while standing up, thus allowing the pelvis full rotational motion.

Squat with arm lift

Technique: Stand with your feet hip-width apart and turn your toes outwards. Bend your knees and lower down as far as comfortable. Whilst down, drop your arms above your head. When standing back up, put your arms back down by your sides. Repeat 5-10-15 times.
Benefits: This targets your glutes, hamstrings, and quads.

The windmill

Stand up with your arms hanging loosely by your sides. Start swinging both arms upward and around in as wide a circle as possible. Continue swinging them like a double windmill around, maintaining smooth, regular momentum and a wide arc. Perform this exercise 10-15 times. Shoulders must be kept loose. During the downswing, let the chest protrude and the rib cage expand fully. The windmill exercise limbers and loosens chest muscles to facilitate breathing. Heart and lungs are open and stimulated, enhancing breath control.

Abdominal Lift

Technique: While standing up with feet shoulder width apart, lean forward and place hands on the thighs just above the knees, with thumbs next to fingers along the inner thighs. Exhale completely and immediately pull the entire abdominal wall back toward the spine and up into the diaphragm. By emptying the lungs first will facilitate this upward thrust of the diaphragm by the vacuum. Then on exhalation let the organs fall back to their original position. Do this a few times, by pulling and letting go of the abdominal.
drawing
Benefits: This amazing exercise squeezes stagnant blood from the internal organs like water from a sponge. It strengthens and tones the diaphragm, it improves its flex, thus facilitating deep breathing.

STRETCHING - Exercises

Loosening exercises are focused primarily on the joints. Stretching concentrates on the muscles, tendons, and ligaments. The mobility of your body and physical coordination depend entirely on flexibility of the joints and the tone of the tendons, which attach joints to muscles. Energy, blood, and nerve impulses can circulate freely when joints are loose and flexible, and muscles are stretched and relaxed.
The stretching must be done slowly and relaxing. By first stretching the muscles, stagnant blood will be squeezed out, permitting the subsequent relaxation phase to draw in fresh arterial blood. For a more progressive grow rather than compacting the muscles, regular stretching is required for a more supple, rather than stiff, and keeps nerve, energy channels, and blood open and unobstructed.

Stretching must be a part of your everyday workout regimen. Stretching is essential for improving flexibility, which is a vital component of overall fitness, along with mobility, strength, power, and endurance. Especially for those that work in an office where they sit for hours. Flexibility is particularly important for injury prevention.

Flexibility is related to muscle tension and length, and it is a component of mobility. Mobility is the key to functional strength. The stronger you are through a complete range of motion, the more powerful and less prone to injury you are during workout and everyday life. I have been hurt many times while lifting or even performing a sudden back/spine twist for whatever reason. Since I started exercising regularly, I haven't been hurt at all. Because my muscles, tendons, knees/ankles/spines are flexed, limbered, and warmed up every day.

Dynamic stretching focuses on moving joints through their full, functional ranges of motion. Dynamic stretching affects dynamic flexibility, it primes your muscle for action, which is why you want to perform it before a workout. Dynamic stretching stimulates sensory receptors called muscle spindles, which are located in the belly of the muscle. When stimulated, two things happen: The stretched muscle is signaled to contract, and the opposing muscle is signaled to relax.

<u>Cat/Cow Pose</u>

Technique: As a start begin on your hands and knees in table pose. Your hips should be set directly over your knees and your shoulders, elbows, and wrists should be in line and perpendicular to the floor. Keep your back straight (like a tabletop) and your spine in a neutral position. Let your neck be long and your eyes soft, looking at the floor. Stabilize your shoulder blades by drawing them down your back. Once you are on a Table Pose, move into *cow pose* (Figure **A**) As you inhale, simultaneously lift your sit bones upward, press your chest forward, and allow the belly to sink toward the floor.

Lift your head, relax your shoulders away from your ears and gaze straight ahead. As you exhale come into Cat Pose (Figure **B**). Simultaneously round your spine outward, tuck your tailbone and draw your pubic bone forward. Release your head toward the floor, but don't force your chin to your chest.

Go back and forth between Cow and Cat poses on each inhale and exhale, matching your movement to your own breathing. Do this from 3 up to 10 breaths and try to keep an even distribution of weight between your hands and knees. When you are done with the last breath, end the stretch in Table Pose.

COW Pose
(Fig. A)

CAT Pose
(Fig. B)

Benefits:
The cat/cow pose helps tone the gastrointestinal tract and female reproductive system.
It allows more coordinated physical movement.
Improves flexibility.
It acts as an excellent warm-up for the entire body.
Since it actively stretches your back, torso and neck, it improves your spine alignment.
It strengthens and stimulates the abdominal muscles. It helps in regulation of breathing patterns. It stimulates your kidneys and adrenal glands. It is greatly beneficial in relieving back pain.
It helps relieve stress from menstrual cramps, lower back pain, and sciatica. The cat/cow pose stretches and increases flexibility of the neck, spine, and shoulders.

The movement also stretches the muscle of the hips, back, chest, abdomen, and lungs. This pose is a fantastic way to warm up and stretch the spine. Since it's also a breath synchronized movement, the energy flow from the Cow tilt to Cat stretch, has powerful benefits for the body, mind, and soul.

UPWARD DOG Pose

Technique: You'll be lying straight out so find a flat surface (hard surface/floor) and lie flat on your stomach with your forehead on the floor and palms placed flat at about shoulder level. Your torso, thighs, and feet should be firmly planted on the floor with the tops of your feet facing downwards.

Make sure your toes are pointed straight out. They should stay this way for the whole exercise, which will help strengthen your spine. You will be stretching the full length of your body. You don't want to twist your body anyway, or else the exercise won't work properly. Relax the spine completely.

And now raise your head and stretch it back until you are looking upward, then raise the top part of the torso off the floor using only the back muscles for lift. When you reach the limit, continue bending upward by pushing up with your hands until your spine is fully arched. Make sure you don't raise the abdomen off the floor, and also don't straighten and lock the elbows. Hold this position for 20-30 seconds.

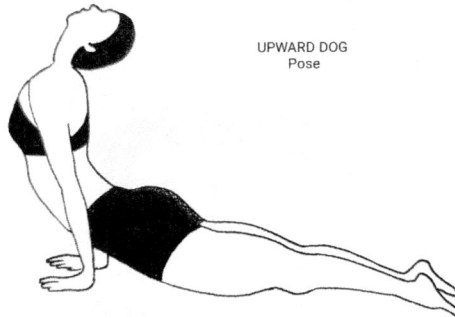

UPWARD DOG
Pose

Benefits: The Upward Dog pose is a simple maneuver that can help stretch your abdominal muscles and strengthen your lower back muscles. To a lesser degree, this exercise also works the muscles in your arms, shoulders, butt and back of your legs. You can also develop greater flexibility when practicing this pose on a regular basis.

TRIANGLE POSE (Tri-Kon-asana)

Technique: Stand firmly on your feet, toes pointing forward. Keep the spine and neck straight. Spread both your legs, (about two feet apart/60cm). Lift your arms up at the level of your shoulders and make them straight, parallel to the floor. The palms should be facing forwards. Your palms, elbows and shoulders will be on a straight line. Now getting into the pose: Rotate the left foot toward the left side. Your left toes will be pointing toward the left, while the right foot will remain the same. With an exhalation, slowly bend your upper body from your waist toward the left side.

NOTE: Make sure your body doesn't bend forward. Without disturbing the line of both arms, bring the left hand toward the left foot and try to touch its ankle. Keep the right hand straight toward the ceiling. The fingers of the right hand should be pointing up, toward the ceiling. Both arms should be straight. Stretch your neck, turn your head up, toward the ceiling, and gaze at the thumb of the right hand. Now inhale and exhale deeply, engaging your core and pulling the naval in. Bring your awareness to the flow of prana (Chee or life force energy).

Hold this position for 10-30 seconds according to your comfort. Once you are done, release the stretch and return to the initial position keeping the arms straight. Repeat the same thing for the other side. If you are a beginner you may not be able to touch your ankle when you stretch. That's ok. Don't worry about it. Make sure you stretch as much as possible and in suitable time you will be ready to reach your ankle with your hand (don't cheat, I'm watching you).

Triangle Pose
(Tri-Kon-Asana)

Benefits: It mainly increases flexibility and strength of the legs and side waist. It mainly strengthens the muscle of the waist, core, hamstrings, thighs, knees, and ankles. It is an effective way to open the muscles of the hips, hamstrings, and spine. This exercise also reduces fat accumulated at the side of the waist. Through the breathing exercises the Triangle Pose helps in reducing mental stress, tension, and depression. The core importance of exercises is so that oxygen/life force energy flows everywhere in your body. When that happens you become healthy physically, emotionally, mentally, and spiritually.

Contraindications for Triangle Pose
1- Do not bend your body forwards. Bend it only toward the sides.
2- Do not overstretch your body. Listen to the limits of your body and stretch according to it.
3- Do not bend the knees when performing this exercise.
4- If you have diarrhea or any other stomach issues, do not practice this as it will stretch your digestive organs further and it can have an ill effect in such conditions

THE PLOUGH (In Sanskrit-HALASANA)
Technique: On a flat firm floor lie down on your back with feet together. Raise your legs up using your abdominal muscles to lift and swing your legs over your head until the toes touch the floor behind your head, or as far back as you can go. Inhale, then stretch farther on exhale. Your knees must be locked, legs straight and your arms stretched on the floor. Stay in this posture for 1-3 min.

Inhale slowly and rhythmically through the nose. At the end of this exercise when you put your body flat on the floor in its initial position, relax for a few seconds and then if you want, you can do the bridge pose that you will see later on to cut down on time.

The PLOUGH POSE
(HALASANA)

Benefits: The PLOUGH pose opens up the neck, shoulders, and back. By compressing the abdomen, it massages and tones the digestive organs, which improves detoxifications. This pose stimulates and regulates the thyroid gland, relieves excess phlegm and mucus, and regulates the breath. This is the best spinal stretch exercise that you can do. Some types of headaches are instantly relieved by this posture because of the brain receiving enough oxygenated blood since the heart will easily pump the blood to the brain with minimal effort.

THE PYLON

Technique: Spread your feet apart in opposite directions of each other, and thighs parallel to ground and your calves perpendicular. Place your hands on your thighs just above your knees. Your spine must be erect, your head straight, and your butt well tucked in. Squat until you stretch the tough tendons and large muscles connecting your inner thighs to pelvis.

Stay in this position until your thighs begin to shake, and then bring heels and toes together to a normal stance. To relax the muscles and tendons, kick your feet out loosely to the sides.

P:S- For a more well around exercise you could do Bellow Breaths (from the Breathing Exercises section) and also practice anal contractions so your urogenital diaphragm can receive an excellent workout.

The Pylon

Benefits: Any cramped muscles and tendon between thighs and pelvis will be stretched by this exercise and energy channels will be opened up along the inside of the legs from the perineum to the feet. The Pylon exercise will enhance your sense of balance and you will feel energetic.

BRIDGE POSE

Technique: Lie down on the floor. You can place a thick folded blanket under your shoulders to protect your neck. Bend your knees and set your feet on the floor, heels as close to the sitting bones as possible. Exhale, and pressing your inner feet and arms actively into the floor, push your tailbone upward toward the pubis, firming the buttocks and lift the buttocks off the floor. Keep your thighs and inner feet parallel.

Clasp the hands below your pelvis and extend through the arms to help you stay on the tops of your shoulders. Lift the buttocks until the thighs are about parallel to the floor. Keep your knees directly over the heels, but push them forward, away from the hips, and lengthen the tailbone toward the back of the knees.

Lift your chin slightly away from the sternum and, firming the shoulder blades against your back, press the top of the sternum toward the chin. Firm the outer arms, broaden the shoulder blades, and try to lift the space between them at the base of the neck up into the torso. Stay in this pose between 20-45 sec Or 30sec - 1 min. At the end of the minute release with an exhalation, rolling the spine slowly down onto the floor. You can combine this with the Plow exercise, meaning perform this at the end of the Plow exercise.

Bridge Pose

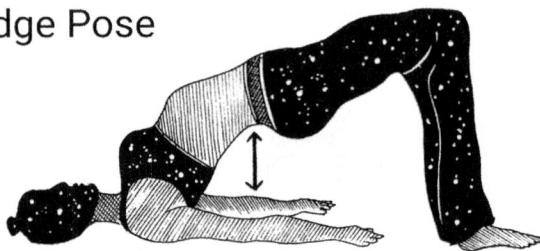

Benefits: It stretches the spine, neck, and hips. It strengthens the back, buttocks, and hamstrings. Improves the circulation of the blood. It also helps alleviate stress and mild depression.

Walking lunge and Dip Splits

Walking lunge challenges your stability, requiring you to engage your core as well as your glutes and legs.

Technique: For the Walking Lunge (Fig. A) Stand tall with your feet hip-width apart and your arms at your sides. Keeping your chest lifted, shoulders back, core braced, and back flat, take a large step forward with your right foot, lowering your body until your right thigh is parallel to the floor, and both knees are bent at 90 degrees. Bring your left foot forward to return to a standing position.

For the Dip Splits (Fig. B) perform the same as for the Walking Lunge, but before returning to a standing position, rock gently up and down 5-10 times. You can alternate between both the Walking lunge and the Dip Splits or perform first a couple of sets of the Walking Lunge and a couple of sets of the Dip Splits.
Drawing of deep splits plus arrows for dip splits and

WALKING LUNGE
(Figure A)

DIP SPLITS POSE
(Figure B)

Benefits: Both the Walking Lunge and the Dip Splits will help stretch your hip flexors. Warming them up for cardio or compound strength-training moves like the lunge and squat. These exercises stretch the large muscles and tendons on the front and outer part of the thighs. It improves balance and stimulates energy meridians between pelvis and feet. It limbers, relaxes, and energizes all major muscles and tendons involved in supporting the head, neck, pelvis, spine, and legs. When practiced in conjunction with the loosening exercises, they provide a complete workout.

LOOSENING - Exercises

SHOULDER ROLL

Technique: Stand on your feet with your arms hanging loosely. Begin rolling the shoulders alternately up, back, down, and around on a 360-degree circle. Roll them as wide as possible in a circle/arc a few times, then reverse direction, rolling the shoulders alternately forward. You may practice this exercise alternately or both shoulders at the same time forward and then both backwards, and one shoulder at a time.

Benefits: This exercise limbers the tendons that attach the shoulders to the sockets. It loosens the joints.

PENDULUM

Technique: Stand with your feet parallel, shoulder width apart and your knees locked. Bend forward until your back is parallel to the ground. Let your arms and head hang loosely down. Twist the entire torso from side to side, causing arms and head to swing back and forth like a pendulum. When twisting, use only the hips and lower back muscles. When you perform about 10 or so 180-degree swings from side to side, stop twisting the torso and let the pendulum gradually decrease, swinging until your arms come to a full stop. Repeat this ten-swings set two or three times.

Benefits: This simple but amazing exercise limbers the vertebrae, neck, spine and the joints of elbows, wrists, and shoulders. It also the energy meridians running from the spine into head, and from the shoulders down to arm and legs.

JUMPING ROPE - Cardio intensive exercise

If this is the first time you are reading this book and are thinking of doing rope jumps right away, read first the description at the end of this exercise where it says "**ATTENTION.**" There are diverse ways/exercises for cardio such as running outside on the treadmill and more. But I'm only going to mention my favorite cardio exercise is jumping rope especially in the winter or in any other season when there are no possibilities to run or use a treadmill. Also, jumping on a rope barely requires any space. I suggest you don't do this exercise at the last hour before sleep as at that time you will want to calm your body and mind and not awaken it for an intense workout.

Technique: Not that any technique is needed but as a start jump as if you were to gallop for a few times so the heart's muscles start warming up and then you can jump with both of your feet at the same time. Or start jumping with both your feet if you wish, as long as you have been warmed up first. At the beginning go at a slow speed and increase gradually. Do this exercise a couple of times a day or more times if you wish.

Each time do 30-50 rope jumps and take notes of total jumps in a day as it should motivate you to do more. Numbers are just a reference as everyone is at a different body/mind health level. Or maybe you have an injury or bad knees which of course you should skip this exercise. If you do have leg injury, then you can exercise your heart by swinging the arms in front of you fast as if you were to be running at full speed outside.

you are running without moving your legs. Just picture how your hands, arms and shoulders would move if you were to be running fast. You emulate that same movement, and your heart will beat faster which is what you want to do. Providing you have no heart conditions, otherwise you should seek medical advice (homeopathic doctor of course). If it was me, I would not seek advice from a mainstream doctor that gets paid by those that profit on us being sick.

Benefits: Strengthens legs, glutes, calves and improves muscle tones in both the lower and upper body. It improves mood, heart of course, brain health and increases body density (not fat). Jumping rope for 10-15 minutes a day burns major fat and calories. I do 400-800 rope jumps every day. Before I started to exercise regularly, I couldn't do more than 50 without having to stop from heavy breathing. I was not fat either.
After a while exercising, my stamina was building up, and I can easily do 500 a day (not at once, but in sessions). At once I usually do 120 jumps. I can do more but I play it safe for my heart. What is safe for me may not be safe for you. As always numbers here are examples.

ATTENTION-Cardio exercise or any other intense workout (*ONLY Rope Jump* exercise is an intense workout in this book) must be performed after you have been warmed up very well first.

The most important part of not doing any intense workout without having warmed up first is that your heart will take the hit, especially if you already have a heart condition. Even if you don't know or think that you don't have any heart problems, it doesn't mean you don't have any. Look around you, we are surrounded and bombarded by poison through air, water, food, and technology. So, to be safe, warm up first.

LONG LIFE - Exercises

These are named Long Life Exercises because they promote longevity. These exercises extend the functional of various vital organs, glands, muscles, joints and other parts of the body. You can practice these anytime, anyplace. Breathe rhythmically and naturally during the exercises. You may pause and take a few breaths when you feel you need a recharge of Chee energy.

Hip Circles (bump and grind)
Technique: Stand with your feet hip-wide apart, knees slightly bent, hands on hips. Move your hips in a clockwise circle as though you were swinging a hula hoop around your waist. Make larger circles as your muscles warm up. Continue for 20-30 seconds and then repeat in a counterclockwise direction. You can also perform the same exercise but instead of keeping your hands on your waist, raise them up above your head so palms are facing the sky or the

ceiling.
Draw with hands on waist or above head or both
Benefits: This exercise loosens up the back, hips, and core.

Standing quad stretch

Technique: Stand with your feet hip-width apart, use a furniture or wall for balance if necessary. Keep your chest lifted and core braced, bend your right knee, and lift your foot behind you, grabbing the top of it with your hand. Actively press against your hand to feel the stretch in your thigh and hip flexor. Release your leg and repeat with your other one.

Benefits: Tight quads (usually from prolonged sitting) can contribute to lower back pain by tugging on your pelvis. This flexibility exercise prevents that by stretching the front of your legs and hip flexors.

Anal Sphincter contractions
I believe a drawing is not needed for this exercise.

Technique: This exercise can be practiced standing, walking, or sitting. Inhale and briefly retain the breath, while performing a quick series of deep anal sphincter contractions. Hold the last contraction for a few seconds, then completely relax the sphincter as you exhale. When lungs are empty, perform one more deep contraction and release it before beginning the next inhalation. Do this 2-3 times.

Benefits: This exercise expels noxious gas and helps prevent constipation. It exercises the urogenital diaphragm and provides an excellent prostate massage for men. It prevents the formation of hemorrhoids by flashing out stale blood from the anal sphincter and associate muscles and eliminates energy and blood stagnation from this vital point.
Helps men gain control over the urogenital canal, for use in ejaculation control, and helps women gain voluntary control over the vaginal love muscle. For pregnant women, this is an effective way to prepare the pelvic muscle and tendons for childbirth. Practice this everyday anytime of the day.

Head and Neck twist
Stretch the neck and direct the eyes straight ahead, unfocused. Turn the head 90 degrees to one side by twisting the neck around until both eye can see the shoulder. Repeat this 10-15 times. Keep the exercise soft, do not stretch very hard. This exercise limbers the muscles and tendons pf the neck and cervical vertebrae, which stimulates the nerves there and massages the thyroid and

larynx.

Stretching and rolling Tongue

Begin to stretch the tongue out of the mouth as far as possible 5-6 times. Then roll the tongue around the mouth clockwise along the external gumline a few times, then repeat counterclockwise. This exercise stimulates beneficial salivary secretions from the ducts below the tongue. These secretions should be swallowed to benefit digestive functions in the stomach. These secretions contain powerful enzymes that help eliminate bad breath. The tongue muscle is directly connected to the heart muscle, which means that this exercise limbers the heart.

Ear Press

Press palms tightly against your ears and abruptly pull them away. Repeat a few times. This balances air pressure in the eustachian tubes and ear canals. Relieves ringing in the ear and alleviates certain types of headaches

Finger acupressure

Massaging at this spot sends energy up the arm channels into the head, stimulating the brain. Since it lies along the channels that control the large intestine, it helps regulate this important excretory organ. You can find the spot by probing your thumb deeply into that soft depression until it strikes a point that is sharply sensitive to pressure. Press this point 10 or so times on both hands.

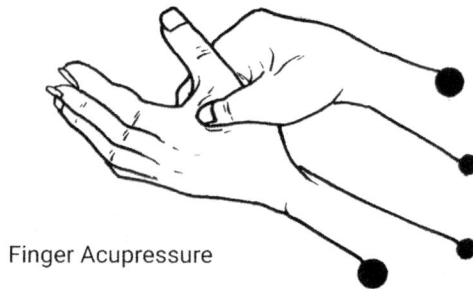

Finger Acupressure

Benefits: Pressing at this spot, sends energy up the arm channels into the head, stimulating the brain. by massaging this spot, it relieves many types of headaches and toothache on the side that is pressed.

INNERGATE POINT

Technique: This little exercise can be performed while sitting, lying or standing. The precise spot that must be massaged is located 2 inches from the wrinkle that marks the boundary between the bottom of the hand and the inner surface of the wrist and directly between two tendons of the wrist. Firmly press at that area until you find the spot that will be sharply sensitive to pressure. Massage that spot a few times or so.

Benefits: Pressure here stimulates circulation and helps regulate heartbeat. This is the best point on the body to use for emergency treatment of heart attack. This is the best thing to do before it's too late for other measures.

Face Rub

Do this either sitting or standing. Start rubbing the palms of your hands together briskly to generate heat and draw energy into the palms. Rub the index and middle fingers in circle around the closed eyes for about 10 times or so. Repeat the same procedure but now around the ears. Then rub again the hands and place index and middle finger on either side of the nose and rub briskly up and down between inner corners of the eyes and lower corners of nostrils.

Benefits: Rubbing the palms together, charges them with Chee. Rubbing around the eyes with charged palms, improves the vision and enhances blood and energy circulation to the eyes. Rubbing the sides of the nose draws blood and energy to the sinuses in preparation for breathing exercises. The nose rub is an excellent technique in the winter for preventing head colds.

RELAXATION

You may be someone that finds it exceedingly difficult to totally relax your body and mind even if your practice deep breathing daily sessions. There are two postures that can induce total relaxation of body and mind permitting all muscles, ligaments to totally relax and unwind like springs released. These two postures can be practiced at any time of the day. They can give you a quick relief of stress-related muscular tension.

Head Hang

This posture is easier and doesn't require as much time as the next pose (The Corpse). Especially when you don't have much time or if there is not quiet in the house for long periods of time. You can practice it before going to sleep. But in the morning, it must be practiced after or before a workout routine. This posture focuses especially on those muscles responsible for the most frequent forms of nervous and muscular tension. Especially the region of the upper spine, neck, shoulder, and upper chest.

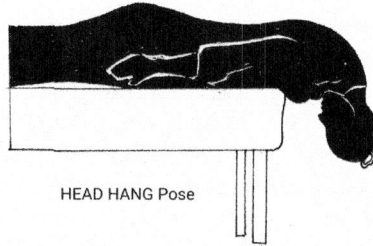

HEAD HANG Pose

Technique: To perform the HANG HEAD posture make sure first that you are not wearing clothes that constrict your blood flow such as tight pants, shirt, collar, hat, belt. Lie flat on your belly on your bed or across a table or a desk so that your head hangs freely over the edge. Keep your arms flat against your sides on the bed. As neck and shoulders muscles gradually unwind by gravity (or by being heavier than air-Flat Earther here), your head will hang further down and feel heavier. Inhale and exhale slowly and naturally through the nose. Hold this posture for 2-10min

Benefits: This posture stretches and limbers the back of the neck, where chronic tension in many tiny tendons and muscles located in the neck, translates into all sorts of problems especially nervous disorders and fatigue. This kind of stretch opens up the energy channels there, drawing Chee (life force energy) into the brain.

NOTE: This pose is fine for a few minutes a day. But not for a long time. There are people out there that stand on their head (as an exercise) for 30min-1h. That long might damage your fragile nerves. You were not created to stand on two fit unnecessarily. Blood never enters the brain in large quantities and in full force but in sufficient quantity to keep the brain working.

THE CORPSE (Shavasana)

Technique: Lay on your back on a firm surface, or bed if the mattress is firm. Let the arms and legs drop open. With the arms about 45 degrees from the side of your body. Make sure you are warm and comfortable. If you wish you can place a blanket under or over your body. Close your eyes and take slow deep breaths through the nose, breathe in fully (use all your lungs' capacity by breathing with both the diaphragm and the chest) and slowly exhale until your lungs are empty and then repeat.

A full complete breath is by first breathing with the diaphragm(belly) and then keep breathing by using your chest until you can't breathe anymore. And only then begin to exhale until lungs are totally empty before beginning to inhale again.

To know if you are breathing right and in order (first belly and then chest), put one hand on your belly and the other on your chest. Make sure that the belly rises up first when inhaling, and then the chest.

As the body relaxes, feel the whole body rising and falling with each breath. After 2-3 min of conscious deep breathing, release the control of the breathing, mind, and body. Let your body move deeper and deeper into a state of total relaxation.

If you'd like to listen to the music, make sure it is just instrumental as songs with lyrics will keep your mind awake. Practice the corpse posture anywhere from 5-15 minutes. When you decide to end the session and release, slowly deepen the breath, wiggle the fingers and toes, reach the arms over your head, and stretch the whole body, exhale, bend the knees in the chest and roll over to one side coming into fetal position.

Remember the part where you should not get up right away without warming up when you wake up? It applies the same here, after you are done with the corpse posture. Since you will be totally relaxed, the blood (part of it) goes to the pancreas/liver for purification. So, to not put any stress on your heart, warm up like you would if you just woke up from the night sleep.

The point is to make sure the blood (which carries oxygen) is fully everywhere in your body before you lift up your body from the floor/bed. The little secret is to make sure the heart has adequate blood and oxygen before having to work against gravity (do not have another word to describe gravity, lighter than air but that's three words).

Contraindication- On the third trimester of pregnancy you should not practice the Corpse Posture as you should not lie on your back for a prolonged period of time. In the third trimester the uterus becomes heavy and can press on the vena cava, a large vein that runs to the right of the spine. Compressing it can restrict the blood flow to the heart, making the mother dizzy, and to your baby.

Benefits: Corpse pose is essential to practice at the end of every YOGA practice. This posture rejuvenates the body, mind and spirit while reducing tension and stress. You should feel all relaxed. It can also be practiced at any time of the day without you having to exercise before or after. You may be away from home, so anywhere you may be is good, provided you find a flat surface and quiet environment.

When this is done at the end of an exercise session, it is traditionally followed by a seated meditation period to re-integrate the body-mind-spirit back to the world. Performing the corpse posture before, is to calm the body before practice. You can also just sit and meditate for a few min before doing the posture. Depending on how strong mentally you are.

P.S. - Yoga is a fancy word for "EXERCISE." Although different styles of exercises have different names, the purpose is the same to rejuvenate the body and calm the mind.

Leg Up Pose

This simple posture can also relax you, whether after workout or just by itself during the day when you feel you need to relax and release tension. This is quite simple. Just lie down on the floor (carpet) with your legs up against the wall or furniture. Hold this posture for a few minutes. Put a folded towel or blanket below your lower back if you wish.

LEGS UP Pose

Any posture that the heart is on the same horizontal level with the heart or lower than the heart, will greatly help your body benefit from the simple fact that the blood will freely flow to the brain. The heart does not have to overwork against gravity. Do this posture at least a couple of times a day.

Chapter **FOUR**

EATING

I t is remarkably simple, just consume fruit, vegetables, nuts, and grains/ herb. Products of nature. Consume only products that grow from the ground. Consume it at its rawest form. The moment the product is tampered with, its benefits will be diminished. If you have to cook something, cook it lightly so as to not destroy the live active enzymes, proteins, and fiber that is in the food.

Raw fruit is the best healthy diet in my opinion based on personal experience and based on proven studies of a great dietitian that challenged any mainstream doctor to prove him wrong about fruit diet. He proved that all diseases happen as a result of a body full of mucus. His name is Arnold Ehret.

> *"If you have eaten wrong for 30, 40, 50 years, thereby producing your disease, you must do the necessary compensation as preparation for your sins: you must do the opposite by eating clean, natural, divine food, which will produce health instead of disease." -Prof. Arnold Ehret.*

Two delightful books of him that I suggest are:

"Rational fasting" and *"Mucusless Diet Healing System"*

Last meal to be at least 2 hours before sleep. Do not drink water while having a meal because while eating, your mouth produces saliva/active enzymes to break down the food. If you drink, you wash down those super important digestive enzymes. For some foods is fine but for others not as the later ones will have to be broken down completely in the mouth. Remember that the stomach does not have teeth.

The farther from its natural form a food is, the more energy is wasted by your body to digest it. Soak your nuts overnight (do not think dirty) so you can give easier time to your digestive system. Fruit is highly detoxifying food. It removes mucus. You have mucus in your body, even though you may not think so.

When you have a runny nose or phlegm, know that is mucus that the body discharges. Mucus is the body's natural defense against infection, but in excessive amounts it can actually have an adverse effect by harboring bacteria and other nasty things in your body. This can in turn, cause sickness.

The lymphatic system moves excessive stagnant mucus out of the body and higher amounts of fruit (along with a healthy diet) help to aid this process. Aim to consume food within the same group. For example: In the morning consume only raw fruit. For dinner, consume a big raw veggie salad. If you must consume cooked food, then do not mix it with food that does not take long to be digested such as raw fruit and vegetables. Do not mix raw food with cooked food. Better to eat a cooked meal by itself and on the next meal consume raw food. In Digestion Times below you will innerstand the why.

STAGNANT OR FREE FLOWING ENERGY

Everything you eat and drink has a vibratory resonance. What you consume, affects your vibration, either lowering or raising it. If you feel blockages while trying to communicate with your guides (metaphysical/unseen-for those that don't know what guides are), it means that you must focus on unblocking stagnant energy. Low vibration energy becomes stagnant. High vibration energy simply flows in accordance with divine creation.

If your goal is to ascend to higher states of being and become light, you cannot consume low vibrational food and reach this goal. It is all about vibration. What you eat, has direct affect on your spiritual vibration. Look at an animal, to see its consciousness.

"All animals have consciousness. The higher the consciousness of the animal is, the more it will affect you after eating it."

The higher the consciousness, the more it will pull your vibration down from what it normally is. Animal's vibrations are lower than that of the humans. When you consume animal meat, the vibration of that animal will remain with you for about 72h, holding your vibration down for the duration of the 72h.

Combining this with the benefits of fasting (the 72h mark), should tell you how important is to reach that 72h fasting mark. But even if you don't have meat, your vibration could still be lowered by smoking, processed food, fear, worries, grudge, not letting go, envy etc.

Here is a list of the common edible meats so you can have an idea of the different animals' vibration.

High vibrational affect
10 Bear
9 Beef – Deer – Elk – Buffalo – Horse

8

7

6 – Goat

5

4 Chicken – Turkey – Emu – and other Fowl

3

2 Rabbit – Alligator

Low Vibrational Affect

1 Fish*

0 Lobster – Crabs * (no vibrational affect)

*Fish can even be worse than eating pork. Consuming fish, spikes mercury levels in the blood. It takes the body approximately 100 days to detox 50% of the mercury. Mercury takes up to 27years to leave your brain. Imagine how long it takes for the vaccinated people to be clean of all the mercury and other poison that the jabs contain. Let alone that most have multiple vaccine injection throughout the years.

A mothers would have to abstain from fish for about 5 years to avoid exposing her fetus to heavy metals and pollutants from fish. **Since mercury accumulates all over the body, women should get their hair tested before getting pregnant**. Mothers who had more fatty acids from fish, had children with delayed language development.

*Even if lobsters/crabs have no vibrational affect, they are grown with chemicals that will affect you spiritual progress, just as the fish are.

Those that hunt animals for sport, instill fear into the animals. Fear is low vibration and it will be in the animal, therefore will be passed onto the person eating the animal. You will notice that on the list you will not see Pork, Cat, Dog, Whale and Dolphin. If you are on a spiritual path, **Pork, Dog, Dolphin, Cat** and **Whale** are an absolute **NO**. Eating this animals, will stop your vibration from growing completely and it will surely bring your vibration down.

Be aware that even if you do not eat meat, meat substances are in many packaged food so I greatly suggest you do not consume any food that is packaged. They are made with the purpose to make money off you and to make you sick. Some products are more dangerous than others.

Even if you don't feel sick when consuming certain products that doesn't mean that you are not sick (low vibrational consciousness). A disease doesn't have to be visual/physical. A disease is also invisible such as mental, emotional and spiritual. But, eventually these invisible diseases manifest physically as in cancer and many other diseases that you know/heard about.

The reason that our vibration lowers when we eat meat is that we are not allowing the animals to leave in harmony with creation. The Universal law of Love dictates that they be allowed to exist in harmony. If you eat them, that is not harmony. You took away their sovereign right just as what the controllers of the world have done to humanity for a long time by taking away the sovereignty.

Although nobody can take away your rights unless you allow your rights to be taken away. But you might ask that what about when animals eat each other in the wild? Well, that is fine, that is in accordance with the law of love, which means that they have to learn love and compassion (their consciousness. Bigger animals eat small animals. Their spirits occupy each other through different reincarnations so that they learn lesson, so that they start learning the beginning of the emotions. You too have been an animal in the distant past, whether you believe it or not. If you think this is ridiculous, that means that you identify your self with your name/personality in this lifetime.

As I have written in my 1st book I AM THE KEY THAT OPENS ALL DOORS, that you are not your name, your social status, your gender etc. This life you are living is simply a test, a game, a school. It is all about overcoming your emotions. Have you noticed that in this world some people behave like animals? That is because their consciousness is very low. It means that either they have regressed so much through their eating, thinking, talking, doing choices, or perhaps they are the 1st generation of the incarnation from a previous animal consciousness. To wrap it up, eating animals is a **NO**. You might eat those animals that are low danger from that list, but they still contribute in the overall energy/consciousness level that you will have. The choice is always yours. No judgment as far as whether you eat meat or not. I love you all. I simply write with the genuine intention to make you aware of the fake reality and the true reality, the one that you and only you have the key to manifesting it. Manifestation happens both ways. Manifesting low vibrational life or a high divine one.

DIGESTION TIMES

How long does it take for the food to leave the stomach? We have been conditioned to eat and drink without a second thought. Most people eat for pleasure and not to enjoy the food and most importantly they do not pay attention to what they eat, how to eat and why they eat. Below there is a simple chart of various kinds of foods and the time it takes for them to be digested. Follow/remember these principles to prevent rotting and to maximize digestion, absorption, utilization, and elimination.

Time it takes to be digested and leaving the stomach.

Water - Right away
Juices & teas - 15-20 minutes
Raw fruit - 20-40 min
Raw vegetables - 30-50 min
Starches - 1 hour
Grains - 1.5 hour
Legumes - 2 hours
Nuts & seeds - 2.5 - 3 hours
Meals that are properly combined (no meat or fish) *- 3 hours
Improperly combined meals - 8 hours

*By properly combined means combining raw fruit varieties with raw vegetable varieties. Do not include starches (with exception of vegetables that have starch such as potatoes, or grains or nuts) because based on the chart above combining the raw fruit and vegetables with the other foods will increase the time that it takes for the foods to be digested. You might say that it is not a big deal if food takes 20min 1h or 8 h.

The more time that it takes for the food to be digested, the more energy your system has to use, therefore it will be many hours before your system has all its 100% energy back for healing. Your energy should be used to be healed and not to digest constantly and increase chances to get sick. Remember this important thing that no matter how healthy raw fruit and vegetables are, if you combine it with foods that take much longer to be digested, the raw fruit and vegetable will be mixed with the other food and stay in the stomach until the rest of the food is digested.

Which means that the fruit and vegetables will ferment. When fermentation occurs, then mucus starts forming. Mucus is the culprit/enemy in everyone's bodies. One other thing to have in mind, is to chew your food until it becomes like a liquid before swallowing, as your stomach does not have any teeth. That is why your teeth are for.

Meat is the one that takes the longest to digest. Eliminate it from your diet. There are plants that give you vitamin b12 (my favorite B12 intake is **nutritional yeast**) and any other nutrients that you think you are getting from it.

Meat is loaded with antibiotics (**antibiotic=Anti Life**), puss, lab made chemical so-called food to feed the poor animals. DO NOT consume food that has a nervous system which includes both meat from animals and fish. Give at least 30 minutes before drinking water after the meal.

And don't drink water no later than half an hour before the meal. As that will conflict with the digestive process. It will surely disrupt the digestive process where complications will arise in the long term. Eating is not for healing.

Eating is to detoxify the body to the point that the body will heal itself. You can't heal your body. That is your body's job. Your job is to make sure that your body is in the right conditions so it can heal itself. And the best way to achieve that is by consuming raw fruit as it is the best detoxification food. And of course, fasting.

Raw fruit is the best most beneficial food to eat. Water that is contained within fresh fruits and vegetables, is not just H2O. It is actually alive/living and structured water. It carries a charge called chemically as H3O2. This (H3O2) is the fourth phase of water, also known as exclusion-zone water. H3O2 is neither solid nor liquid. It is more like a gel-like substance, found intracellularly in the body.

Your body converts H2O to H3O2. It is immensely beneficial to consume fresh raw fruit and vegetables, especially fruit. It hydrates you at a cellular level. It is far superior than any water out there. Consuming raw fruit and vegetables is very important daily and also before fasting, especially when you plan to fast for long periods of times.

BAREFOOT WALK

Walking 1-2 h per week can add years to your life. We are designed to walk. If we do not walk, the blood doesn't flow regularly, it will concentrate in the liver. Not enough oxygen will go to the muscles, blood, organs etc. Since we know beyond doubt that oxygen means life, then not walking at all or enough we set ourselves up for premature aging. Walking improves memory, reduces depression, it can cut obesity by half.

Even if you are not obese you must walk. Even if you never get fat, it does not mean that you are healthy. Walking is beneficial to both physical and mental health and it can be done anywhere, it burns calories and simply feels good. Even if it is raining outside you can walk in the house, it is what I do. If you live in a house that has floors, then go up and down the floors a few times and you will see your heart pumpkin faster which is good.

The blood and brain (and the whole body) get oxygenated, but also the heart muscles get exercised. If you suffer from anxiety, just by walking regularly, should help reduce it. If you can (I do not see a reason why not), listen to the music when you practice any kind of exercise. For two reasons, one because music is food for your soul, without music there cannot be life. And second by listening to the music you are focused mostly on the music instead of analyzing the surrounding.

Walking is greatly beneficial. Just like a car that will be powerful when it is running, also your body will fill up with energy. But if you do not walk/exercise, is like being in a parked car, dead, lifeless. The bottom of your feet has acupuncture points/meridians, and they get massaged when you walk barefoot.

Or when you massage them with your hand. Different spots of the bottom of your feet are connected energetically with your internal organs and other areas of your body. It's even better if you walk barefoot when it's sunny outside. Sunlight is very important, especially in the fall and winter.

SUN LIGHT THERAPY

The sunlight must reach the retina of your eyes, whether you look at the sun directly (directly **ONLY** at dawn and at dusk) or during the day as long as you are outside for at least 1h total in a day. If it is not sunny or cold outside, you can get a sun lamp. As it will mimic the natural sunlight. In Japan it is what they use in many offices and the workers feel great as they receive the natural and not artificial light. Sun lamps are used to help regulate the *circadian rhythm* – a biological clock that sets the time for the sleep-wake cycle and hormone release.

It function best when it is synced up to the natural rhythm of light and dark. It is very important to go outside daily as the light from the Sun will send a cue to your body that it's time to be active and alert and help keep your circadian rhythm in sync. Light Therapy Boxes are used to get the body clock back on track and improve mood, sleep, and energy levels at the same time from the comfort of home. Especially in the winter where there is not as much sun as other times, this is very helpful and beneficial to you. Sitting in front of a sun light for half an hour a day can be very beneficial to you.

Everyone has a slightly different circadian rhythm and depending on the person, to some it may be more beneficial to sit in front of the sun lamp in the morning, and for others may work best in different times of the day. So, to be sure practice this light therapy 2-3 times a day, in different times of the day.

Sit about 30cm away from the sun lamp but don't look at it directly. For anything in this book that you are not sure or have doubts, do your own research. But always be open minded. As if you are not an open-minded person, then you will tend to believe research that aligns with your beLIEfs which would make you feel comfortable. **You don't grow in comfort.**

READING

Reading is beneficial to organize your thoughts and emotions. It is beneficial to an all-around health package mind-body-soul.

"Every man who knows how to read, has it in his power to magnify himself, to multiply the ways in which he exists, to make his life full, significant and interesting." -Aldous Huxley

Reading 20-30min a day promotes memory retention. Prevents neurodegenerative diseases. It prevents the creation of Alzheimer disease; it also promotes the formation of new neural pathways. Only creativity promotes expansion of neural pathways. By reading, you visualize your body, the past, the future and many other thousands of things whether those are things in the form of memories or imagination.

Both memories and imaginations are made of the same substance Akasha. The ether/air may be invisible to your eyes, but it is not. It is full of things, entities, words/dimensions etc. Your prana/life force energy that keeps you alive comes from the Ether.

"If you have a garden and a library, you have everything you need" -Marcus Tullius Cicero

Don't just read for the sake of it. Reflect on what you read; you do not have to finish a book at a certain time. I see online or offline friends that challenge themselves to read 20-30 books in one year. Who cares how many books you read.

It is important what you read and whether you absorb the information you read or not. Now, of course if you do not absorb some information, it may also mean it is a current information or information way above your level. Just as some books that I have, are kind of difficult for me to absorb. That is because they are of a different level, not necessarily higher level, but different. If you read a book that is a hardcore philosophical book, then you cannot absorb a lot in a brief time because philosophy requires lot of analyzing. I used to lean toward philosophy, and I still do but less as in the level that I am now.

I prefer peace of mind instead of over thinking. Almost all philosophers are conflicted inside their mind because they analyze everything to the most minuscule details. I was like that, and thanks to beginning the path of spirituality, my mind is calmer now. Whatever information you read, reflect on it, and move on.

"Reading without reflecting is like eating without digesting
-Edmund Burke'

"Read so that you can remember what you already know. And when you remember it all, put it in action. You are full of knowledge waiting to be turned into wisdom. Do not doubt yourself. Do not let your ego tempt you with self-doubt" - S.K.

Chapter FIVE

MEDITATION - THE "WHY"

The purpose of meditation is to make your mind peaceful and calm. When your mind is calm and peaceful, you will be free of worries, anxiety, fear, discomfort. A peace of mind is true happiness. If your mind is not peaceful, you will find it exceedingly difficult to be happy, even if you live in the best conditions. No matter the conditions, they are external. Nothing external will bring you happiness unless you have a peaceful mind. By having a peaceful mind, any great external person or thing will be enjoyed as a reaction of a peaceful mind.

Many people expect internal reactions (happiness) as a result of external things/people. It is the other way around. By meditating regularly, you will train your mind to become calmer and calmer, and as a result you will find better solutions to any problem or supposed problem. Technically any supposed problem will disappear because it was not there to begin with. Your messy, cluttered mind thought that they existed. The thoughts will get you closely attached to things and people and as a result you will be disappointed after the temporary joy of those things/people has worn off.

It is temporary because those people have their own path to follow, they will not be with you forever.

The only person that will be with you forever is "you"

Because someone is temporary in your life does not mean that you should get away from them. No, you can enjoy them for as long as they are in your life without having to be disappointed when they depart and continue their journey. You are just one of many of their stops, they will have many other stops (meet other people) until they reach their destination.

How do you enjoy the journey better, by not stopping anywhere or by stopping in many different stops and enjoying sightseeing of different places by also getting experience? By different stops it does not mean about meeting different partners, I don't mean that. Although that is also a way to get many experiences because you will learn different mindsets, emotional behavior, and a myriad of other things.

What I meant is that life is full of beautiful things and people. Enjoy life with all it has to offer. But to innerstand the WHY and the HOW, you better meditate regularly as when you have a clear mind, an inner knowing will be triggered. An inner knowing from previous lives. If you do not have a clear mind, you will barely learn anything in this lifetime. Which would paralyze the inner knowing of your next lifetime.

But regardless of if you believe in reincarnation or not, at least focus on this lifetime to make the best of it, by being the best version of yourself every day. Which means progress incrementally, no matter how slow as long as you progress. If you have a cluttered mind, you will keep repeating the same routine every day. How can you progress by doing the same things every day? Progress requires effort, but it will be effortless when you meditate regularly. A big mistake that many people make when meditating is that they try to stop their thoughts from coming in.

The more you resist, the more thoughts will pour in. Remember the story of the monk and the woodcutter on PART TWO? So, you just observe the thoughts and let them go peacefully. Thoughts create experience when you analyze them. When thoughts pour in just say "hi" to them and do not feed them with your analytical mind.

> "Your thoughts are hungry monsters; they will devour you when they sense weakness."

The more you practice meditation, the more it will happen to you instead of you trying to do something as a chore.

"No other way to achieve inner peace unless you achieve that zero-point energy where there are no analytical thoughts, no judgments. Just pure bliss eternal Godlike experience." -S.K.

Now, I innerstand that we all have families, friends, and children where it is not possible to be at peace 24/7. But I am sure that you can find 15-30 minutes to meditate daily. Get up early in the morning when everyone else in the house is asleep so you can meditate. Or in the evening after everyone goes to sleep. The rewards from meditating regularly are priceless. When you become a regular daily meditator, then you can also meditate while awake, conscious wherever you are, at work, at home etc.

hat I mean is that when you have practiced regular meditation in solitude, then you have learned or mastered the art of observation. The art of observation is simply practicing observation of everything without analyzing, overthinking, or even better without thinking at all. Quiet your mind, get away from delta brain waves that keep you in an anxious, worry lifestyle or should I say deathstyle.

All the struggling or suffering that you have, or that will be going through, it was, is and will be your own doing. A cluttered mind creates all sorts of problems that are not there. When you wake to your true potential, you will clearly see beyond the veil of deception/darkness created by your lower self

(EGO).

"The quieter you become, the more you can hear. You can hear your inner voice, your intuition, your God/Goddess within." -S.K

LAYERS OF MEDITATION

1- Physical Body
2- Emotional Mental/Ego
3- Higher Self Guidance
4- Union/Light Being

Physical Body
You begin meditation. You feel only the physical body. You are still awake at this point, meaning conscious of your physical self.

Emotional Mental/EGO
You go deeper and encounter the emotional self and ego. You will/may have tingling in your body: toes, hands, shoulders, head.

Higher Self Guidance
You clear the emotional body and begin to realize the subtle body and sensations. You are not really conscious at this level. You can ask your higher guidance/higher self any question and you will receive the answer in the form of sensations in your body or warmth.

Union/Light being
You begin to channel light and slowly build your multidimensional body. You are unconscious at this point. You have access to other dimensions at will. You will be unconscious in this dimension that you are now, but conscious in the other dimension.

HOW TO MEDITATE

If you have already decided to meditate and explore the endless possibilities as a result of regular meditation, then you are already on the road to a successful path and happiness. The road may not always be straight and flat. It may get bumpy. It is up to you to avoid the bumps so you can have a pleasant and joyful trip. It takes practice and a certain level of effort as it is something new for you, assuming you never meditated before.

Do not start meditation with expectations. Expectations almost always lead to disappointments. When you don't expect, you receive the ripened fruit. By not having expectations, you have already planted a healthy loving seed that will grow and thrive.

1-Find a **quiet and comfortable** place to sit inside or outside.

2-If you have a **special place** in the house that makes you feel good, then meditate in that spot.

3-Try different spots to meditate, and whenever you find the spot that feels right and make you feel undisturbed, then **always meditate on that spot** as that spot will be associated with your aura, your energetic electromagnetic field.

4-Start meditating for **only 5 minutes** as a beginner. Do not set the alarm as that is not good for your brain. Just stop meditating when you feel like it even if it was less than 5 min. Just check the clock before and after. It is what I do. But I do meditate for at least half an hour because doing it for a while.

5-For the first days and weeks meditate in **short sessions** until you feel comfortable to meditate longer.

6-**Consistency** is the key here. You may have been meditating for eight straight days, but if you skip one day, you undo a lot. You must not skip. I speak from experience. Well, 99% of the content of this book I have experienced. The other 1% only you can prove it, such as seeing past lives or different dimensions which is a personal experience that only you can prove it to yourself.

I cannot prove that to you as it is something that only an individual person has to prove it themselves. Plus, I don't need to prove anything. This book is written with the big assumption/common sense that the readers will do their own independent research and be their own scientist by practicing different things instead of doing what doctors (drug dealers), $cientists say.

"A journey of a thousand miles begins with the first step." -LAO TZU

7- Not every meditator is the same. Either meditate a few times a day in **short sessions**, or less times, or once a day for **thirty plus minutes**. The numbers I give are references, not rules. You do what feels right. If you are determined to become mentally healthy, you will decide how long and how many times you meditate.

8-Before you start to close your eyes for meditation, remain calm, look around you without analyzing what you see, just half observe by keeping your **eyes half closed**.

9-Breathe deep a few times with your diaphragm so you can be in the moment. Even if you have your eyes closed you can still keep breathing deep so you can get into the habit of being in the moment.

10-**Don't try to control** your thoughts, whatever thoughts come in your mind, observe them quickly and **let them go.**

11-Don't plan to meditate for 20 min and expect to achieve results in that time. **Meditate without expectations**. The first few days or weeks (depending on how determined you are about achieving peace of mind) are the hardest as you are not used to it. The brain has to be trained, just like you train a baby or a person at the first stages of their life. When you teach a baby how to walk, how to eat, how to brush their teeth for a while, then they will do it themselves as if it's normal. The same thing applies for meditation or anything else that you start to learn for the first time.

12-While meditating use the floor (sitting on a pillow). This is not for beginners, so I suggest you **sit on a chair or bed**. For longer sessions sit on a step stool and put your back against the wall, furniture, or your bed, that way your spine is supported and helped by the wall/furniture, and you will not feel tired. This way you will be enticed to meditate longer.

If you are a novice meditator, then as a beginner listen to healing frequencies while meditating. Either guided meditation or just instrumental. Whichever you think is more comfortable.

Chapter **SIX**

WHY AND HOW TO FAST

Before fasting (juice or water fasting) you must prepare first by eating for a whole week only raw foods (fruit/vegetables) and spending the last 2-3 days of that week by consuming only fruit. This helps clean the bowels from putrefied matter, flushes the liver and kidneys, and sets the body in the right motion for your fast. This is only if you want to go straight to juice or water fasting, assuming you are already decently healthy, otherwise start with the first level of fasting which is '*All raw food fasting*'.

Do not eat snacks between meals. *The hourly benefits of the fasting* section will make sure you innerstand why it is important to let your body digest properly until the next meal and not indulge in snacks. Consuming snacks while fasting (assuming you would want to cheat), even a single almond or a grape, takes you back to square one. The 1st step to successful fasting is to achieve the 12h mark with no food consumption or juice at all, but you MUST drink lots of water. Don't think that if you haven't achieved the 12h mark or no juice or no food at all is not an achievement.

Just the simple fact of you attempting to fast it is a big feat in itself. The reason why I'm calling it an achievement after the 12h mark is because after 12h of the last meal, the digestive system stops, and it is when the miracles start. Unless you stop the digestive system (after the 12h mark), your body will never have all its available energy to heal itself properly. Fasting can be self-empowering and incredibly fun when consciously done and not when you forget to eat or when you don't eat when no food is available.

The role of fasting it's in helping your body to cleanse and restore itself, and it is proven over and over again. Before you ask me "Where Is the proof", I could very easily pull-out information from books, articles etc, but then you just as easily can find books and articles that say the opposite.

So, I'm telling you that I AM THE PROOF. I have proved to myself and others (directly or indirectly) that you can be your own doctor, scientist (not a $cientist), your own teacher and your own student that you don't have to prove it because we all are students by default no matter how long we live or how many lifetimes we go through. If I showed you proof (whatever proof means to you) then you lose the ability to discern.

"The moment you realize that you are your own doctor is the moment that you become the actor, writer and director of your own life" -S.K.

When the body starts to clean its lymphatic system, the sinus cavities, lungs, and other body tissues will be active in the cleaning process. **You must not stop this healing process** as it is the body's most effective way of getting rid of mucus, toxins, and any other wastes. By letting your body perform this healing process, your body will increase the function of your cells and it will be on its way to regeneration where new healthy cells will be formed replacing the damaged, dead ones.

A big mistake people make (unknowingly of course) is when they have a flu or flu-like symptoms, they rush to the doctor or p**HARM**acy to get treated. Not knowing that these symptoms are the body's way of healing itself, then people suppress this amazing healing mechanism by taking pills/medications. When the body is in the process of cleaning itself, it will purge out toxins, mucus through the nose or mouth.

When people suppress that process by taking medications, where do you think that mucus goes? It stays in the body, not only that but it will spread in other areas of the body that are not sick. Please - let the flu do its course. Listen to your body, respect it and it will reward you. Flu-like symptoms are your body's way of telling you that it is healing itself.

You may have lots of mucus or even some blood with it. Don't panic, as the blood has been there for a while. Your body knows that it has been there for a while, but it will purge it out when your overall system is at a point that something must be done. When your throat is sore it means that mucus and toxins in the tissues are trying to get out. If you must use cough drops, then use natural ones. Imagine if you didn't have any cough or no pain or no fever or any other discomfort, what would happen?

You would die. That is why we have the symptoms. The body is telling us that we are at a critical point to do something about it, to take care of it. If you don't feel good, do not eat as eating will put the digestive system in high gear and there won't be much energy left in the body to heal you. That's why it is recommended to not eat at all when you don't feel good. But water is necessary. If you are a very weak person physically, then while not feeling good, drink juice and water but not just water.

Of course, as always if you are not comfortable following my advice or anyone else's advice for that matter, then go to a doctor if that makes you feel safer because it is someone with a title/degree. But no matter which drug dealer (doctor) or homeopathic doctor you go to, they can only help you to a certain degree. Only you know your body better than anyone else. I will never get tired of quoting Hippocrates:

"If you are not your own doctor, you are a fool"

"Marching through the side effects of fasting, you pave the way to rejuvenation and regeneration"

You don't eat the fruit the same day you plant the seed. Working hard for something is more rewarding than when it is readily available. I will make a quite simple example before moving onto the different types of fasting. Whenever you were sick at one point in your life where you had a flu for 2-3 days or food poisoning, did you think about money, going to the movies, buying any materialistic junk, dancing, or singing etc? I don't think so. That time (while sick) is the time where everyone appreciates life. When sick we realize that money is meaningless, but that is a forced appreciation/ gratefulness for being alive.

And that happens rarely as most people are sick but a bit at a time where they walk, work during the day. Why do you have to be sick to the point that you have to stay in bed for you to realize how important, beautiful, amazing your biological body is. Why not be grateful every moment throughout the day, or night if you are a night bird.

Fasting is the remedy of remedies. When you give your digestive system a break by only consuming juices (home made ones and not the junk ones from the store), your body begins to use all the pranic energy to achieve higher levels of consciousness by awakening the pineal gland and the crown chakra.

While fasting it is easier to attract/manifest. While fasting, your psychic powers unlock and your intuition strengthens. Begin fasting and discover the powers that you possess. The unseen realm will slowly be revealed to you and you will not want to go back and indulge in food that is designed to keep you a morta

To anyone attempting to do a long fast:

You must walk, jog, soft exercise/stretch daily. And also practice the **INNERGATE POINT** *exercise under* **Long Life Exercise** *section, that is connected with the heart. Also roll your tongue (**under the same section as the one above**) clockwise and counterclockwise for 10sec respectively along the outer wall of the mouth. It limbers the heart because that muscle is connected directly with the heart. You must put effort to be healthy.*

The effort must be joyous and not a chore. It is joyous when you want to live your life instead of just existing. To live a comfortable life you must live it uncomfortable. Which means 1st you put effort, getting out of self-destructive comfort zone and after the effor, you get rewarded with comfort. When you enjoy life, the effort becomes the new true comfort that you must function daily by putting effort in anything you do by engaging with love. When you engage with love about anything, you create heaven. ***Effort turns into LOVE.***

<u>All Raw Food Fasting (BEGINNER)</u>

Well, this cannot be really considered a fast if you have to eat. But to those that consume heavy food, meat, alcohol, processed unhealthy food (if you want to call it that - "food"), might as well be considered a fast. Animals do not cook food before eating, only humans do and those (Nephilim) that taught humans to. As a beginner, take this one day at a time, consume only raw food for the whole day.

One day a week only raw fruit and vegetables. In the next weeks try two days per week (or keep going at only one day a week for 3-4 weeks and increase incrementally), not consecutive as you are not used to it yet. For example, raw fruit and veggies on Monday and repeat the same thing on Wednesday or Thursday. This is just a simple guideline.

Everyone handles things differently. You may try two consecutive days if you can, or three days a week depending how determined you are, or if you are already on the road to healing. Most people's bodies are loaded with mucus, puss, and antibiotics, lab made chemicals etc. Even if you don't take any antibiotics prescribed by the drug dealers (doctors), it doesn't mean that you are not consuming any through the regular chemical-filled packaged foods you buy in the store.

Depending on the severity of your disease (by just walking and not feeling any pain, does not mean that you don't have any conditions), do not consume raw fruit and veggies the whole week as a start. The reason for it is that fruit and veggies are the best natural detoxifiers, and they will detoxify you so fast in a truly short time that your liver will be flooded with toxins, and that is not safe. There are people that get sick after changing their lifestyle from eating mindlessly to eating and thinking mindfully. And that is because a big change happens in the body.

The body goes into withdrawal. It happened to me years ago when I totally changed my diet. And because was/am a very deterministic person I cut many foods at the same time from my previous crappy diet (which I thought I was eating healthy).

We all think we eat healthy because we are accustomed to consuming certain foods regularly. But as soon as we start to change our diet then we have no choice but to realize that we were not eating healthy after all. In my case I did not go back to eating unhealthy food, I kept continuing my healthy diet and after a short period of time of not feeling good, my body adjusted to the new type of diet which was raw fruit and vegetables and occasionally cooked vegetables.

This type of fast (if you choose so) must include raw fruit, raw vegetables, water, and fruit juice (homemade), or organic fruit juice that you buy in the organic store. Pay attention at the back and front of the fruit juice package (assuming that they are being truthful). Some packages say organic juice. Yes, it may be organic, but where does the juice come from?

The fruit itself or they add flavor that smells and tastes like the fruit? There are many ways to deceive customers, so it is better that you make yourself the juice in a blender. It is cheaper (in the long run) and healthier as you would not add any chemicals and also because you will make it with love and not for money. The food you buy in the store is grown for money therefore, no love went toward the product.

When you follow this diet, besides the juice made from fruit, you can also consume the smoothie made out of the fruit, this way you don't have to throw away the pulp. While you do this type of fast, don't consume any type of protein type foods such as nuts or seeds. The reason for it is that nuts and seeds take longer to digest, the longer it takes to digest food, the more energy is used by your system which the energy used up for digestion would have been used to heal many other areas of your body.

Nuts and seeds are super foods but the purpose of you consuming only raw fruit and vegetables is to clean out and detoxify the system. But if you want to eat nuts, then eat them by themselves, do not combine them with other foods. Based on the chart of how long it takes for different groups of food to leave the stomach, eat the nuts after the fruit/veggies have left the stomach.

Refer to the chart (about how long it takes different kinds of food groups to leave the stomach) so you get into the habit of knowing when to or not to eat or combine foods. And also soak them over night. Before becoming healthy, you must first stop taking what makes you unhealthy. But one thing at a time. When you practice this level of fasting or when not fasting, it would be wise to eat fruit as a first meal of the day, as fruit, is water and it cleans the bowels and also it does not put any strain on the digestive system form being relaxed all night or when you break the fast anytime.

The more hours/consecutive days you fast (this is about water or juice fasting) the more days you should consume fruit before starting with heavy vegetables as your system is cleaner, calmer. How would you feel if you started to run as soon as you woke up? Your body would go into shock, even if you wouldn't feel it. You could even die if you do extreme running or exercising as soon as you wake up without having warmed up and stretched properly. Yes, you could even die.

Of course, depending on your age. But even if you are young, the damage will be done to your heart and the damage is accumulative. Many deaths could have been prevented if people knew that simple fact about their body. You could even die if you ate a steak or a boiled-up potato after a medium or long fast. A potato is sticky gluey starch and can clog/lock your bowel up. I don't intend to instill fear but better to know and be prepared with knowledge and innerstanding than be consumed by ignorance.

Water is one of the most important things to your survival, but you can choke with it, you can drown in it. Fire can warm you, but it can also burn you. What I'm saying is that what is bad or good, healthy, or unhealthy, is our knowledge, innerstanding, reaction and application of that knowledge.

**Anything that gives you "life",
can also take it away from you.**

I was going to use the saying *"everything in moderation"* but it can be interpreted differently by different people. Just like I have heard people telling me that they consume alcohol, cigarettes, medication, and processed food in moderation. I'm not sure whether to laugh or cry over that kind of irresponsible ignorant statement.

To wrap up this first level of fasting, I will say that for any kind of fasting you must do it gradually, meaning take out of your diet one bad thing at a time and add 2 good things, so you can be a step ahead. If you are obese or simply fat, then do not start right away all raw as your body is loaded with mucus, toxins, and other poisons. You wouldn't want your liver to go on vacation would you? You might struggle more than others at first as it is the same as trying to skip steps when you go upstairs.

All is possible when you have will and determination. FAT is not a bad word in itself. If you get offended by it, then that's on you for letting a word be more powerful than your will to become healthy. Only weak people get offended by words.

ALL FRUIT FAST (INTERMEDIATE)

Before moving onto this next level, you must have tried and been successful at consuming for a whole week all-raw fruit and vegetables. All-fruit fasting is very highly recommended for the simple fact that we are frugivores. **This type of fast is harmonious with our physiological and anatomical process.** All fruits are good but the most highly recommended fruit to consume are grapes, melons, and watermelons.

They must be organic and seeded. In the case that you cannot afford organic, then non-organic which is a lot better than any other processed food. At least the fruit grows from the ground (Mother Earth), although the soil is depleted of rich nutrients. Make sure to thoroughly wash the non-organic fruits as they have high levels of pesticides and herbicides. Make sure to eat melons by themselves without combining them with any other fruit as this fruit will just go straight through the small intestine without having to go through digestion.

Grape or grape juice fast is a proven remedy for cancer. Proven not by the western medicine of course. Western medicine thrives from sickness of people. Grape juice fasting is normal in Russia. Oh, and in Russia GMO food is not allowed.

Juice Fasting (EXPERT)

Start this after a whole week of consuming only raw fruit and vegetables. Juice fasting is the easiest (between juice and water fasting) as the juice from fruit contains nutrients, fiber, vitamins as opposed to water fasting. You can last longer while juice fasting, but after a while of practicing this level, it will be much easier for you to last long even when water fasting. **This is high level fasting which gives your GI (gastrointestinal) tract and digestive tract a rest**.

This type of fast is a very high-level energy fast that stimulates much-needed cleansing and lymphatic movement, while keeping your kidneys flushed out throughout all duration of the fast. Juices supply glucose and fructose to cells for energy, that's why you can last longer and easier while on juice fasting as opposed to just water fasting.

You can either fast on vegetable or fruit juice, but the real power is in fruit as we are frugivores. There are always exceptions of course. If your pancreas is damaged from cancer or otherwise, it will not digest food so whatever you eat it will come out undigested so in this case fruit juice is the best option because there is only little effort for the pancreas to process the fruit juice.

After a while, the pancreas will improve, and you can introduce vegetable juice in combination with fruit juice. And you can heal it completely with fasting. Not just the pancreas but any organ can be healed. As always as you believe, so shall it be. But of course, belief by itself will not heal you if you keep eating junk.

Water Fasting (HARDCORE)

This is the hardcore fasting. It is difficult if you don't do it consciously and with intention. For water fasting you should consume only reverse osmosis or distilled water. Your digestive energy is totally given to the immune, lymphatic, and glandular systems as opposed to the juice fasting where the immune and digestive system have to use the energy because the juice still contains very small chunks of fruit which they still must be digested.

A high level or body cleansing and purging is done by fasting only on water. Your body is designed very intelligently, it is full of wisdom and will focus on removing stored toxins, inflammations, and mucus.

Water fasting is not recommended for those weakened individuals with depleted energy levels. **If you are a very highly depleted (of energy) person, you must not practice this type of fasting as it could lead to death**. To be safe, the highest you should go is *all fruit fasting*. As a beginner try to water fast for 24h, and then increase the duration of fasting. During a fast the body will use stored fat as energy. Most people have plenty of that.

Don't worry as you will not starve. You may get hungry but not starve. It's all in the head. You be the boss; the stomach must listen to you. Fasting stimulates new cell growth. It should make you feel younger. Not at first as you are making a big change. When fasting regularly there will be inner unity as water is LIFE.

Dry Fasting (GOD LEVEL)

ATTENTION: I do not recommend this type of fasting (yet, unless you have 1st practiced the other ones) because it is dangerous. Do not get discouraged by the word dangerous. How many foods, drinks that you have consumed all your life that are dangerous? A lot. You didn't think (or were clueless as I was a long time ago) them as dangerous because they took your life a little at a time incrementally. Just like if you put a frog in a pot with water and turn on the stove, the frog will not leave the pot as he will be boiled gradually in it. But if you put a frog in the pot with already hot water in it, then the frog will jump right out.

Dry fasting cannot and should not be practiced when you are a beginner. You must have already been practicing water/juice fasting for a while before attempting dry fasting. Leave your ego and pride aside and do proper research before attempting this kind of fasting. To practice dry fasting means that you have already achieved a mind/body/soul balance that you can nourish yourself just by being in the sun and by just breathing properly the Chee (life force energy) energy that always exists in the Aether/air.

It may sound ridiculous to you but yes, it is possible. You might ask that if I do not recommend this type of fasting, then what's the point of writing about it? I write about it so that you know that there is more to your amazing body than what you have been led to believe. Plus, I do not know the level of each reader.

Many people think that they are living a healthy lifestyle for them to discover that that is not true at all. It also depends on what your purpose in life is (at least on the health side), to live a long and healthy life or to achieve immortality.

It takes 30-48 hours of dry fasting for your intestinal fluids to become completely at equilibrium, meaning that they are full of strength, and this is why you were told by $cience that you will **die** * by day three without water.

WHY?

Because after 48 hours (day 3), the intensity of these fluids and their healing and destruction of damaged cells in your body, will feel like death to you if you've never experienced it before. You may then not trust yourself and run to the doctor$. The body never harms itself, nor will it do anything to set off harming of the body, ever.

* Some people may die from dry fasting because their mind cannot handle the body's transition back to pulling most of its H (hydrogen) and O (oxygen) from the air. Do you recall these simple elements (H & O ? It is a simple process. When we push our water-addicted, life-long protocol out by forcing the body back to its natural state of water-deprivation from the air, we feel what is close to death, because the body creates vast autophagy (incineration/ destruction of cells).

Due to the intense healing, you initiate with your strong will, and you feel that pain, as autophagy is like cancer, it is a form of cancer. Most do not seem to have the trust and love of their own self, to get past this massive hurdle. But there are some very determined people that do. When the autophagy takes place, the body creates brand new white blood cells which means regeneration. Which means you become younger and stop aging. Similar effect is felt when you transition from a dense diet (meat, processed food, pasta etc.) to a light diet (raw fruit/vegetables or when you just water fast.

You feel like you are dying and that's because many toxins are purged at a rapid pace and body reacts to the pollution. In a way you could say that the older self is dying and a new YOU is reborn.

NOTE: *I recommend that you don't practice dry fasting if you ejaculated in the last 3days. Ejaculation robs you of your life force/strength/nutrients/ stem cells etc. You shouldn't ejaculate anyway, like you will find out in the chapters:* **SAVE GOD'S ELIXIR** *and* **ORGASMING WITHOUT EJACULATING-SEMEN RETENTION.**

Also, before dry fasting, make sure that the previous 3-4 days you had only raw fruit and/or homemade fruit juice/water.
No sex either. Unless you are having cosmic love with your partner where the orgasm is internal and not external/superficial.

◆ ◆ ◆

IMMORTALITY

Immortality can be achieved by:

1-Being expert in fasting on a regular basis*

2-Expert in meditation

3-Losing the mind (the one that society/system gave you)

4-Unlocking and balancing all chakras

5-Waking up the serpent (kundalini)

6-Free of any attachments, be it things or people

7-Achieving light body/vehicle (**MER-KA-BA**)

*Fastin on a *regular basis* doesn't mean every day, it means once in two weeks or once a month. Personally, I fast for 36h in the middle of each month and 72h on the 1st of every month.

It depends at what level of your JOURNEY you are, based on however many lifetimes you have lived so far. Your intention may just be to live healthy and long or to achieve immortality. Immortality doesn't necessarily mean physically, although that can be achieved. When you achieve immortality, you retain the memories of your past life, so you won't have to learn from scratch on the next.

Immortality cannot be achieved by operating on two stranded DNA. All 12 strands must be activated and work in harmony with the Cosmos and everything that the Cosmos has. My DNA has been already activated, meaning more than 2 strands until all 12 will be. Yours are starting to get activated also. There is no way that you want to learn and empower yourself by just being locked in with just two strands.

Being immortal doesn't mean that you will stay forever in the same body. No, although you can live for hundreds and thousands of years in the same body when you are fully/totally aligned with creation. Being immortal means that from one reincarnation to the next (and all other next reincarnations), your memories of the previous lifetime will be intact. You will retain all the experiences/knowledge of any previous reincarnation.

Do you imagine if you remembered everything from previous lifetimes? Well, if now, all of a sudden you would remembered everything, you would stop functioning because your brain/system could not handle millions and billions of experiences/memories. I am talking about when you are conscious. On a subconscious level/DNA, you already have in you all the memories of all of your thousands and/or millions of lifetimes.

To reach the level where you would function without any problem when remembering everything, you must reach a certain level of consciousness expansion. You must reach Christ-like level or 5D consciousness. That is a level when you operate totally from a place of love, gratitude, forgiveness, acceptance etc.

Numbers 4, 5, 7 have not been explored at all in this book. They will be explored/explained in a future book that I will eventually release as they are subjects that need a thorough explanation. By following and practicing the content of this book you will also work automatically toward #4, 5 and 7. But I will leave those (the elaboration) for the near future. Although you can find anything on the internet or other books, you may want to know, or maybe you like my way of interpreting/explaining things. Up to you. Any book that I write is for you. Monetary gain is secondary.

BREAK THE FAST

What is "a breakfast?"

Breakfast means "Break the Fast." Breakfast it's the first food activating the digestive system after however many hours you slept at night without eating anything all night. So, it doesn't matter when you eat. You can break the fast at 10am, noon or even 2-3 pm. It's important what you eat that matters. The first thing you eat will affect the response of two major things:

1- **Hunger hormones**
2-**Gut bacteria**

So, whether you eat the right, or the wrong food will set the stage for cravings, energy levels and your mood for many hours. The first thing you eat every day, no matter what time of the day that is, is particularly important to get right. Most people have no idea what a big difference their gut health and the right food can have on the quality of their everyday overall health! The above section applies the same whether you break the fast from a night sleep, or when consciously fast during any time of the day or night.

It is in the word BREAK-the-FAST. We associate the word *breakfast* with the first meal at the beginning of the day. But breakfast is just breaking the fast so that's why it is super important what you eat after the fast which should be fruit.

When to break a fast? Good question, thank you for asking. The best time to "break" a fast is by you discovering and by listening to your own inner guidance/intuition. Your body is yours; you know it better than anyone. Don't let anyone tell you otherwise. You will know when you fasted enough. Don't fall for times when there is a desire to eat something. Push harder than you think you can, it's how you beat hunger or anything for that matter.

If you break the fast the first time that you feel hungry, you are distancing yourself from learning the best discipline that exists. Controlling hunger is the best discipline. When you learn how to control hunger, you can control anything. Really ANYTHING. After you read the hourly benefits of fasting and innerstand the why, then you can push yourself harder when you look at each hours mark, as it should make you go further because the further you go the healthier you become.

Do not expect immediate results. Everyone has a different pace. One crucial thing to have in mind is BELIEF. If you don't believe that you can then you won't. If you believe that you can, you will. Simple as that. AS YOU BELIEVE, SO SHALL IT BE. Just this simple universal law I just wrote (in capitals) can change your life if you flow with it.

> *"Believing (downstream) or not believing (upstream) being possible, are both sides of the coin you have with you at all times. It is the river of life, flow with or be consumed by it." -S.K*

Usually after 2-3 days of fasting one will lose the desire for eating because the body is starting to use that digestive energy for cleaning and healing. Remember when I mentioned about cheating (you do actually cheat only yourself) by eating even a single grape while fasting?

After 12h of fasting your digestive system stops and all available energy (100%) will be used for cleansing and healing. If you do eat a single grape or anything, even an almond, the body gives a signal to stop cleansing/healing and go back to digesting the food. So, by just eating a single grape you lost all the hours and now the body starts from the beginning process.

Many so-called doctors will say to eat snacks between meals as long as there is balance, but what they don't tell (assuming they know) is what I described above about the importance of not eating snacks at all while fasting. Any time from the end of a meal to the beginning of the next meal it is FASTING.

Or doctors (drug dealer, God I love using this word to describe them) tell you, to eat raw fruit and veggies after a meal but what they don't tell you (I'm still assuming they know) is that raw fruit and veggies shouldn't be consumed after a cooked meal. Throughout generations it is ingrained in people's brains that it is healthy to eat fruit or veggies after a meal.

And that is completely WRONG. Why? I'm so glad you asked again. It is wrong because raw fruit and vegetables are so easily digestible by your body that they must be consumed before a cooked meal or anytime as long as it is not after a meal. Why? Now, I know you didn't ask but I'm glad I have to answer anyway. When you eat a cooked meal, it takes hours for the food to digest, so, if you eat fruit and veggies after the cooked food, the fruit/veggies will stay on top of the cooked food or mixed with it, it doesn't matter, it cannot be easily digested as the cooked food is priority now.

And what happens if fruit and veggies stay for a while in the stomach? IT WILL FERMENT, and it will turn into mucus, *BINGO*. **Mucus is the culprit for any disease**. Throughout the fasting period if you feel hungry a second time, then it is a sign that you should eat. It depends how weak you are. If you salivate easily just by looking at food, then you might be hungry only after a few hours after you start fasting.

Fasting must become a way of life just as breathing is, although many don't breathe properly. It takes effort to breathe properly in the sense that it takes discipline and make it a habit just as breathing improperly is a habit for most.

FASTING IS MUCH HEALTHIER THAN EATING HEALTHY

You have full control when you fast. When your vessel is empty, you are in control. When you fast, you have control of your breath. When you have control of your breath, you are the manager of your heart beats. Having control of your heart beats, means that you have control of your nervous system. And having control over your nervous system, means that you absolutely have control over your mind. The secret to a long, happy, healthy life is having control of your nervous system.

Break the fast with conscious breathing before you put any liquids or solids in your stomach

Chapter SEVEN

THE HOURLY BENEFITS OF FASTING

Innerstanding how different stages of fasting work will/should make you more motivated. Only a person that has given up on life will not act immediately with passion when opportunity for progress/ enlightenment arises. Innerstanding and appreciating the beautiful temple (body) you possess, it's an amazing feeling. Be proud to have been born and witness the amazing, biological vehicle/body you carry around wherever you go. Work with your body, it's your best friend. It's the best relationship one can have.

0h - 2h
BLOOD SUGAR RISES.
You will feel normal during the first hours of fasting because your body is going through the regular process of breaking down glycogen (a form in which glucose is stored in muscle and liver tissue. In other words, it's the substance that is deposited in bodily tissues as a store of carbohydrates). Your blood sugar rises. Your pancreas releases insulin to break down glucose for energy (innerG) and stores the extra glucose for later whenever it's needed.

2h - 5h
BLOOD SUGAR FALLS.
As a result of the effects of insulin, your blood sugar decreases to near normal after spiking. And it typically doesn't continue climbing because insulin is immediately delivered into your circulatory system after eating. Don't be tempted by the grape

5h - 8h
BLOOD SUGAR RETURNS TO NORMAL
At this stage, your blood sugar levels return to normal. Feeling hungry? Your body is reminding you that it's been a while since your last meal. However, you are not actually that hungry. Starve to death, shrivel up and lose your muscle mass? None of this is going to happen. Actually, your glycogen reserves will begin to fall, and you might even lose a little body fat. Your body will continue to digest your last food intake. It starts to use stored glucose for

energy and continues to function as if you will eat again soon.

8h - 10h
SWITCH INTO FASTING MODE

8 hours after your last meal, your liver will use up the last of its glucose reserves. Now your body goes into a state called gluconeogenesis, which indicates that your body has switched into the fasting mode. Studies show that gluconeogenesis, a metabolic pathway, results in the generation of glucose from body fat instead of carbohydrates. It increases your calorie burning.

10h - 12h
BARELY ANY GLYCOGEN LEFT

The glycogen reserves are running out. As a result, you may become irritable or hungry. Just relax, it is a sign that your body is burning fat. With little glycogen left, fat cells (adipocyte) will release fat into your bloodstream. They also go straight into the liver and are converted into energy for your body. Actually, you are cheating your body into burning fat in order to survive. Hide the grapes or the almonds :)

12h - 18h
KETOSIS STATE

Now it's the turn of fat to fuel your body. You are in the metabolic state called ketosis. The glycogen is almost used up and your liver converts fat into ketone body - an alternative energy source for your body. Fat reserves are readily released and consumed. For this reason, ketosis is sometimes referred to as the body's fat-burning mode. Ketosis produces fewer inflammatory by-products, so it provides health benefits to your heart, metabolism, and brain.

18h - 24h
FAT BURNING MODE BEGINS

The longer you fast, the deeper into ketosis you'll go. By 18 hours, your body has switched into fat-burning mode. Research shows that after fasting for 12-24 hours, the energy supply from fat will increase by 60%, and it has a significant increase after 18hours.

1-The level of ketone bodies rises.

2-Ketones act as signaling molecules to tell your body how to better regulate its metabolism in a stressful environment.

3-Your body's anti-inflammatory and rejuvenation processes are ready to work.

24h - 48h
AUTOPHAGY STARTS

At this point, your body triggers autophagy (which literally means self-devouring). Cells start to clean up their house. They remove unnecessary or dysfunctional components. It allows the orderly degradation and recycling of cellular components. During autophagy, cells break down viruses, bacteria, and damaged components. In this process, you get the energy to make new cell parts. It is significant for the cell's health, renewal, and survival.

The main benefit of autophagy is best known as the body turning the clock back and creating younger cells. Which means by fasting from this level to 72h fasting, you slow down or stop aging. You chose- grapes/almonds(or any other snack) or rejuvenation. You know, I'm being funny with the grape/almond example, don't you?

48h - 56h
GROWTH HORMONE GOES UP
Your growth hormone level is much higher than the level at which it was before fasting. This benefits from the ketone bodies production and hunger hormone secretion during fasting. Growth hormone helps increase your lean muscle mass and improves your cardiovascular health.

56h -72h
SENSITIVE TO INSULIN
Your insulin is at its lowest level since fasting. It makes you more insulin sensitive, which is an especially good thing if you have a high risk of developing diabetes. Lowering your insulin levels has a range of health benefits both short and long term, such as activating autophagy and reducing inflammation.

72h - Congratulations if you made it this far (both in reading and fasting for 72h).
IMMUNE CELLS REGENERATE

"*Survival of the fittest.*" Your body turns down cellular survival pathways and recycles immune cells that are damaged when fighting viruses, bacteria, and germs. In order to fill the recycled/not available cells, your body regenerates new immune cells at a rapid pace. It starts the immune system regeneration and shifts cells to a state of self-renewal. Your immune system becomes stronger and stronger. Do you now innerstand how important fasting is?

> *The act of fasting, triggers a switch to flip in the body, signaling it to begin a 'stem-cell based regeneration of the hematopoietic system.' It requires the body to utilize up its stores of glucose, fat, ketones, as well as starting to break down a large number of white blood cells. The loss of white blood cells flags the body, in turn, restores brand-new immune system cells.*

No wonder humanity is plagued by disease and suffering, because if the body is not healthy, the mind cannot be either. Humans eat way more than they should. Do you see how your body can regenerate itself? Provided you put your body in the right condition. Now that you innerstand the amazing process of self-healing that your body goes through, you would have to think twice about what to eat, when to eat, and how to eat and whether you have to eat some days or not at all.

You should aim for 72h fast because at this stage your cells will regenerate at a rapid rate and your slow down or stop aging.

Stopping aging must be done in   conjunction with everything else. Read, absorb, innerstand and apply the knowledge so that you can live a life where suffering can be a thing of the past. At the time of this writing, I'm at 63h mark. Nothing can stop me and nothing can stop you either.

CONGRATULATION!

You went back in time and met your younger self.

Update; I added this paragraph 6 months after I released the book, so I have managed to fast for over 90h. See? I didn't die as many people think would happen if you do not eat for a long time. As always, do your own research. Human body is very complicated, only you know how much you can handle. But always push a little bit more than what you think you can handle, and you will realize that fear kept you from unleashing the potential of your body.

Chapter EIGHT

SAVE GOD'S ELIXIR

T his section may seem to be mostly about men, women must also read it as it is important to innerstand their weakness and support them in regaining their strength. Fasting doesn't only mean to abstain from eating food, it also means to abstain from negative thoughts, negative emotions and also one very important thing to abstain from, is SEX (mostly for men), or if you don't abstain, then make sure you do not ejaculate/waste semen.

And if you are a woman, mention to your partner/husband the super importance of not ejaculating. If your partner watches regularly porn, then it will be difficult at first for him to take in consideration this particularly important thing. And if you (the woman) watch porn regularly, it will be difficult for you to consider this advice for your husband as whichever of you watches adult content is conditioned to think and have certain expectations visually. I am going to assume you get what I mean by visually. The semen is CREATOR's elixir.

You are also a mini creator given the same abilities as the creator but on a micro-COSMIC level. The semen contains very important beneficial minerals that are of a great importance to your health. If you waste the semen mindlessly (not that wasting it mindfully would be possible or logical), you halt the activation of your DNA to a higher frequency. It also diminishes brain neural pathway growth/multiplications. It is not possible to waste it regularly and be intelligent at the same time. (Being smart and intelligent are two different things).

Not only because of not receiving those critical nutrients/minerals that semen contains, but it also contains the Life Force Energy (innerG, inner Chee). Why do you think the dark powers (those behind the scenes that actually make the big decisions) flooded the internet/TV-Paid channels) and magazines with porn and sexuality? To control you of course.

They don't have to control both of you, as long as they control one partner, then that partner will control the other one directly or indirectly. They planted the seeds of destruction in one of you and automatically the other partner or husband/wife watered the leaves instead of taking care of the roots. By planting the rotten seed, the seed will grow so intelligently that the person slaughters (metaphorically) him/herself.

If you are a female, you must at least have to have had sex with your partner as a duty, or to shut him up and be done with it. That happens either because he would get mad/angry or because you are of a certain culture that you have to please him no matter what. Or because of whatever your answers are from the questions below. Or it could be for another reason that only you know.

Questions to women:

- Where would his anger/disappointment come from?

- Where did his urge come from? Porn? Other women?

- Did you please him to be done so he could leave you alone?

- Did you please him out of fear?

- Did you please him out of jealousy so he wouldn't get sex from someone else?

- Did you please him because maybe you are guilty of something you have done and kept it a secret from him?

- How did that work out for you?

- Did having sex without your initiation fix your relation overall?

- Do you have to please him because of whichever religion he worships in?

Questions to men:

- Do you think she is your property?

- Do you need to have your fix regardless of how she feels at the moment?
- Do you watch porn?

- Do you flirt erotically with people you know or those that you don't know (online or offline)?

- Did you know that after a period of time of regularly watching pornographic content you will damage specific neural pathways in your brain permanently?

- Do you cheat with someone that you having a good time, and to keep that good time alive, you require/demand sex from your partner when you cannot have it from the other one?

Even if you are single but watch that kind of adult content, you are getting damaged regardless. The only difference between you and those that are a couple is that you will only bleed on yourself. Temporary gratification is an illusion that you pay with your life. You may not die but if you are not intelligent and not capable of even controlling your own desires/emotions, then it is no different than being dead.

When you depend on sexual desires, you operate in low vibrational energy, and you also become less intelligent. This is a FACT. Just as operating in fear regularly it also lowers your intelligence.

"Your DNA is the Creator's signature."

One gram of DNA holds over 200mmillion gigabytes (GB) of data. This advanced system of living information gives you the capabilities that you have. Only a few know that minerals play an integral role in DNA activation, and that the human body cannot access abilities inside the DNA without an ample supply of minerals. Genetically modified and minerals depleted food supply and porn are part of a plan to keep you in a **weakened** state, so the other 10 DNA strands won't be activated.

The word weakened sounds phonetically like the word weekend. How does humanity feel after the first five days of the week working and giving their life force energy to the CORPorations? -WEAKENED. That's why the last two days of the week are called a weekend/weakened. The English language is very, very tricky and it is not a coincidence.

The best weapon they have to dumb down society (especially men), is through "pornography". If you are a woman and think that if most men lose by wasting the golden mine (semen) that you don't have to worry, you are wrong. You lose too. First you **lose the protector.** Do not be naive and think that you are independent, and you don't need men, as you do need men just as much as men need you. All the emasculation of man is done to take away their protection off you. The fabricated (man-made) laws are created as such to deceive you and think that you don't need man.

Many women rely on the state for protection. But I ask you: Who does the state (government) protect you from? Men? A concrete proof that the government doesn't care about women is the fact that they want to jab (inject poison) men and women and children. Since I'm writing this book in the middle of the pLandemic had to use this example. Let's assume men are dangerous, who made them dangerous and how? The authorities made them, of course they didn't point the gun in their head.

They introduced alcohol, drugs, guns, fake news, porn and so on. All these weaken the state of mind. When a man is not himself, he doesn't know what to do, where to go. In that case, women would be nurturing them. But they wouldn't as the damage has already been done, both genders are separated through mind control schemes. The damage I'm talking about is that of separation through racism, genders, social status, nationality etc. Men protect women, and women nurture men. They both need each other.

But in the current state the separation between both genders is high, but it will change, especially when men's feminine aspect of self-returns. A man without the feminine aspect of himself is lost. I'm speaking from personal experience. We wouldn't have any wars if men knew who they truly were/are. Beside losing the protection, you also lose by just being in their proximity. If their aura is damaged, weakened, so will yours when in vicinity of that person, let alone if you kiss each other, and even worse when having intercourse. Why do you have to pay for someone that cannot control the urge for sex? You may be a man reading this and thinking I take a woman's side. Far from it.

I am writing this chapter this way from the feminine aspect of me that got returned. It was lost through many years of conditioning from family, friends, co-workers, and anyone else I encountered. Now, I innerstand how important it is that both men and women innerstand the importance of supporting each other unconditionally. Women have been suppressed for many generations. Do you know why that is? I give you 5 min to think about it. Never mind, I'll tell you right away. Women were suppressed precisely because of empathy and nurturing. They didn't want women to nurture men. **THEY WANTED MEN TO BE LOST AND NOT KNOWING SELF.**

No woman would ever send anyone to fight in war. No woman would send their children to their early grave. Empathy and nurturing is also part of men, the feminine aspect. They suppressed women so their men wouldn't be awakened to their true multidimensional state of mind. Would you go to war if you innerstood that the person that you could kill is your sibling? Of course not. SO, throughout many generations they groomed women to think and beLIEve that their purpose is to bear children and please their man.

But what they kept a secret was the importance of abstaining from sex, or if not, at least not wasting the elixir. Men mindlessly throughout history got weakened emotionally, mentally, and spiritually. At the time of this writing, it's been 315 days that I have not wasted a single drop and over 4 years without sex. 4 years without sex is just a result of me not wanting to settle for someone that is not healed as with the knowledge I have now I know that I would get sick if I just had sex with anyone or someone that is functioning in low vibration.

And I feel great, clear minded, focused, determined, strong willed and full of purpose. Yes, this is what the controllers don't want men to find out (among other things), the power of semen retention. Now, you may be in a relation/marriage that have children with each other, and for the sake of the children you may stay together or at least one of the partners or both have sex just for the sake of it or without feelings. If there are no children in the middle (or if there are) have the courage to break the patterns that are no longer serving you.

being selfish. But when they are not serving you for your mental, emotional, physical, and spiritual health. You (whichever gender you are) are in no way obligated to stay together with the other person. You do not owe anyone anything. You owe gratitude to everyone (good or bad person) for teaching you lessons but you do not have to stay together if it is unhealthy for one or for both of you. And if you have children together but don't want the children to grow up with only one parent in sight, there is a solution, not the best but a solution, nonetheless.

The solution is a third person in the mix, not at the same time of course, unless you are that open minded, then go for it. I meant when one of the partners or both have someone on the side. Whether you have considered this, or have someone on the side, it doesn't matter. But for this solution to work out you must not be jealous at all, be open minded and have a high self-esteem character.

Yes, it requires nerves of steel. But it also requires open mindedness. Jealousy derives from low self-esteem and the need to own the other person. Ejaculating on a regular basis is **fatal**, PERIOD.

> *Not ejaculating at all is like becoming a God. If you must ejaculate (at least to procreate) do it in spring and not in the winter. Losing that powerful force in the winter is one hundred times more harmful than an ejaculation in the spring.*

Whatever you do, do not have sex when the moon is in your zodiac sign, meaning <u>do not ejaculate at all</u>.

For more information on this, check my other book ***GAIN WISDOM THROUGH PRACTICED KNOWLEDGE***, chapter **SELF MASTERY**. This book is published under my other nickname Rimias K. Neo. I explain in that book the reason why I publish my books under different names.

Chapter NINE

ORGASMING WITHOUT EJACULATING
- SEMEN RETENTION

T his is something that all men should practice. Whether by themselves or with their partner. With the pointing and middle finger of the left hand (assuming you are right-handed) press hard between your anus and scrotum and keep your fingers there. To know what part I am talking about, just when you pee, put your two fingers at that spot and start urinating, stop the pee, let the pee go and stop it again, and you will see that muscle contracting. It's where you should press hard as that place is the canal where semen passes through toward the exit into giving you a surface external temporary pleasure.

Starting 15-20sec before having an orgasm and keep your fingers pressed hard there until 15-20 sec after the orgasm is finished. When the orgasm is finished (with the fingers still pressing), close your eyes, breathe deeply, fully, and visualize the semen going up the spine every time you inhale after the so-called amazing feeling of the orgasm is finished. Keep inhaling and exhaling slowly for the duration of 15-20sec. You will not lose a single drop, **guaranteed**.

This is for when you are single and for when you are in a relationship but when you or your partner finishes you off as long as you block with your fingers that muscle/canal where semen travels. Picture like pressing hard on a hose and not letting the water go through. It's what you do to not let semen go through. Don't think that because you learned this easy technique you will have as many orgasms as you want without ejaculating. Yes, you can do it if you want but this is meant to pave the way toward you beating the urge for sex.

As you still lose power while doing this thing because the **secret of orgasm is that it must be an implosion and not an explosion**. When you combine retention with meditating and eating healthy, you will not have any urge anymore. Not having an urge does not mean that you will not feel like having sex anymore.

It just means that you will control the urge and not the other way around. If you cannot control the urge, then you will easily fall in the trap and may have sex with just anyone that may not be healthy at all, as you won't be able to discern who/what the other person is. Be mindful of not going with just anyone, and eliminate porn (*including looking at naked/seminaked images of people*) from your life.

Watching porn, or having sex with just anyone:

___Will diminish your soul's functionality.
___Will take precious time out of your life.
___Will rob you of your seed, which is meant to only be used for procreation.
___Will suck the life force (**INNER**chee) out of you.

What do you get by focusing externally (watching porn or any other means that has to do with sex/sexualization)?

___You get a few seconds of dopamine rush.
___You get an addiction.
___You get depression.
___You get expectations on sex.
___You have unrealistic expectations.
___You get brain damage.
___You get relationship issues.
___You get erectile dysfunction (eventually).
___You get premature aging.

> *"Excessive loss/waste of semen as a result of frequent intercourse/ masturbation with ejaculation, is the prime cause of impotence in men."*

Is it worth it? It isn't.

It is not worth it at all, unless you are a short-sighted person (*I was for many years*) where you just exist and parasite off of people's blood. But you are not one of them, or else you would have not gotten this book, and definitely you would have not gotten this far in reading it. Your pay big time for those few seconds of dopamine rush (orgasm). You will age faster by regularly spilling the semen. And you will be unattractive to women (from my heterosexual point of view). Sure, some women will be attractive to your voice, smile or to your body in general, but those women are not of a high frequency. So, pretty much you attract what you are.

Depending on whether you're aiming to live a longer healthier life or to achieve immortality where you won't reincarnate anymore on Earth (or Earth-like 3d realm), you must decide whether to have sex (while retaining), or to eventually not have sex anymore. Because sex/lust holds you back. And you will associate with those that hold themselves back, and you could also hold other people back.

Speaking of masturbating, in the book *You Are The One* by Pine G. Land, the author says:

> What is it that you are lacking? Is the intention yours or a result of outside forces or conditioning? Always remember that what is normal doesn't mean that it is healthy or true. The same can be applied for the opposite too, but much less, since in this world low frequency products or activities have become the norm. Your energy must fully flow throughout all your energy centers (chakras) and not be focused only (mostly) on the 2nd one which is the Sacral Chakra. Having the urge to masturbate derives from you lacking real love/sex, or you are too invested in sexuality and that's all you know on how to cope with lack of love. If your keep lying to yourself, you are shattering the truth even further. **The sooner you take responsibility for your actions, the sooner you'll collect the broken shards** (pieces of truths lost along the way).

A few ills that may strike men who abuse their sexual drive are: impotence, anemia, nocturnal emissions (ejaculating while asleep), energy deficiency, anemia, hormone exhaustion. The best cure for the above ills is to frequently have sex with the same woman without any ejaculation of semen whatsoever, several times daily, for 7-10 days in a raw. This is about when you have the diseases mentioned above.

Otherwise, as I have mentioned, you should have sex only if it is on a cosmic level, where you feed each others energies and not deplete. And as always, not ejaculating. The woman thrives from sexual intercourse, it is men who lose. It is how it is. Cannot be changed, it is by design. Those that have all the knowledge of how a human body functions know how to control men that have urges.

Through porn, sexualization of women where in turn the men fall for the trick. If you are the woman reading this, you also have responsibility to guide men to his enlightenment (as far as retaining goes) through encouragement, empathy, will and determination. A man that ejaculates cannot be considered a strong protector being. By design, the woman is the nurturing Goddess and man is the protector God.

Frequent intercourse with no ejaculation is the prime cause of healing from those ills that I previously wrote. This makes good medical sense because nothing in the world stimulates secretion of vital hormones as effectively as sexual excitement. Retaining our sexual energy (fluids/lifeforce) is a must for vitality, freedom and longevity (and immortality if one puts the great effort).

J.J. and TAMO in their book *Rebuild Yourself From Within* state:

"Through our own personal journeys, we can discover the transformative power of semen retention (and *MENSTRUAL RETENTION). By breaking free from the cycle of addiction to porn and masturbation ourselves, we experience a profound shift in our physical, emotional, and spiritual well-being. This newfound awareness enables us to fully appreciate the importance of preserving and harnessing our sexual energy for personal growth and vitality."

*MENSTRUAL RETENTION - I added this part in the above quote by J.J. and TAMO. To read about how to control your blood and eggs/menstruation naturally without any external man-made medication, check the book *Gain Wisdom Through Practiced Knowledge* by Rimias K. Neo

◆ ◆ ◆

Lack of power translates to lack of sexual energy and vice versa

Sexual energy is related to the root/base chakra, the energetic foundation. The deeper the foundation, the higher up you can build. For men, semen retention is that foundation. If you do not have sexual control, you will most likely experience instability in your life. A lot of man (I was one of them years ago) desire to find a woman to "build with", without innerstanding that they must first build from within.

If you always waste away your essence/life force energy through sex, porn or masturbation, then you are depleted, you have little energy to build with. You will not be attractive to strong, high frequency, high self-esteemed women.

You will only attract those women at the same level that you are. You cannot grow with someone that holds you back (or that keeps you on the same level). When you are depleted of sexual energy, you are operating in survival mode. Functioning in survival state of being, will repel women because they need stability and intuitively they know for sure that that's not something you can give them. You cannot give something when you yourself do not have enough. By having lack of sexual energy, you tell women that you are a man who lacks power.

They can easily sense that. By not having power it does not mean that you are weak physically. You can go at the gym every day and be all muscly, but that means nothing when you lack healthy, abundant life force essence. Avoid/reject sex, masturbation. Avoid even watching content that may make you want to have sex. As they are etheric contracts that may lure you in the destruction of your self being.

Unless it is real love, unconditional where both partners give each other 100% freedom, where they empower, water each other. Usually, people are so encapsulated by lust when they see a physically attractive person, that they immediately create assumptions, they assign a meaning behind it. They create a fantasy about this person being a potential partner. All of us have fallen for this. That is because we are not emotionally balanced, we are ruled by our sexual urges and so we rush in irrational thinking and decisions. Think that physical looks don't have a meaning at all, so that you can calm down your lust, think rationally and make definitive successful healthy decision for your physical temple.

By having regular ejaculations, your mind will not be functioning properly. You would function only with basic desires which don't require any healthy, critical thinking. And if you are already in a relationship, you would ruin that relationship, as you would want to have sex, disregarding the other person feelings.

Ruining a relationship doesn't just mean that there must be a breakup, separation, or divorce. Many couples are together, but they are lonely and there are many reasons why they stay together, regardless of if the relationship is a loving one or not. After a while of not spilling your seed, test yourself if you are strong enough to go close to having an orgasm and then stop. Just remove yourself from sex. Try it, by yourself or if you are with a partner.

> It is when I confirmed it to myself that I reached the max level in sexual discipline. I am very healthy sexually, and at the same time, I am strong enough to stop right before the point of no return. This is a result of me having retained for 16 months.

As far as not ejaculating while having intercourse, that is a bit complicated, requires breathing technique and constantly squeezing that perineum muscle. I have not mastered that yet, as I will not practice that with just anyone. I would only do that with someone that is of a high frequency, and not with someone that needs healing (from a *life-long trauma*). I cannot teach something that I have not mastered yet.

But anyway, do this easy thing I just taught you and you will see that you will never waste it, unless you want to have children, of course you will have to use that elixir to plant your baby ;). After a while not wasting it, you will be

stronger emotionally, spiritually, mentally and you will be attractive to your partner as you will radiate energy of strength and protection. The *minerals/ nutrients of the semen* will travel back up to the spine (and also be absorbed in the blood) onto the brain and nourish it.

When the brain is nourished properly, then it will give the proper signals to every other area of the body be it physical, emotional, or spiritual. When both woman and man vibrate on the same level then sex becomes magical. I will close this chapter with:

> *"External orgasm is the silent death, while internal one is the soundful life." - Saimir Kercanaj*

If you do not believe in reincarnation, then you will not innerstand the above quote. The above quote that I created does make sense although at first glance it may not. Do not confuse the word sound with silence. Silence can be the biggest sound there is. The word silent in the above quote is temporary and superficial. While the internal sound (silence) is an orgasmic implosion that echoes into the universe.

You know when you have an orgasm, you lose your consciousness for a moment. A portal opens when you have an orgasm, a portal into a different dimension. And just like here, also in other dimensions there are good and bad entities, so when you have an orgasm, any entity can slip through the portal that you opened. So, that's why it is very important to have sex with someone that you love (that person must be in love with you also).

And if you are a single person, then use your imagination about a person in your life that you loved and got loved. Do not use as an imagination someone from a past relationship that you suffered as you will bring the low vibrations back into your consciousness. For an easier control of the muscle, practice daily the Anal Sphincter Contractions exercise from the **Long-Life** exercises section.

> *Do not give in to external pleasure urges. Just practice this simple technique to retain and you will be on your way to discovering your true potential.*

Become disciplined enough to not be controlled by your sexual urges. When you achieve the capability to control your lustful urges and the urge to eat unconsciously and without purpose, then you'll know that you have become a God. It is the ultimate strength, to be able to control your urges, your emotions, your body.

Discipline is all it is required. Be aware of your limits, and increase every time that you are about to give up. Technically you don't have any limits. Your belief that you have any, makes it so. I can go indefinitely in retention practice. You can too, with the exception where you have to have children.

Nothing can stop you when you have the will and determination. I did it.

<u>You too, can do it.</u>

GUARANTEED

Chapter TEN

OBSERVATIONAL AND THOUGHTLESS (CONSCIOUS MEDITATION)

T he enemies of progress are at all times present or non-present depending on your level of every day behavioral patterns. Those enemies are invisible, not material. But they manifest materialistically in different forms that are detrimental to your life and those that you encounter since anything you say or do will affect the whole universe.

It will affect those you meet directly and the rest of the universe indirectly, because anyone that you affect, with create more actions/behavior based on your good or bad intention. You may not have a bad intention, but when you don't practice the **Universal Law of Cause and Effect**, then your behavior will create bad outcomes and good outcomes. It's a 50/50 chance.

But when you innerstand and consciously practice the Universal Laws, then you direct your life consciously will 100% success. Here, look at the monsters that are residents in your mind that operate from the shadows.

The enemies of progress:

Fear, Anciety, Complaints, Hope*, Expectations, Loniless, Lust, Impatience, Anger, Lying, Worry, Greed, and much more.

*HOPE is an enemy. It makes you lazy. Hoping that things will turn out to your convenience, it's what has tricked many people. Hoping for something without any action is meaningless. Be a doer.

By practicing the Universal Laws, you master the art of Observation and Thoughtless.

> *"When you become the observer and not reacting on things/people that are out of your ability to control, nothing bothers you anymore, because you innerstand the secret of not wasting energy on things you have no control of". -S.K.*

When you truly meditate, you don't even think of these low vibratory negative life sucking EGO traits although HOPE may seem like positive on the surface. The real powerful person is the one that meditates/is an observer while conscious throughout the day with the eyes open and not only when meditating sitting with eyes closed. Because during your everyday life you will be faced with different things, people, situations, or all kinds of vibration such as the ones in the above grid. You are already an amazing creation, given mental, emotional, physical, and spiritual bodies all at once. Balance is required from all four bodies.

God gave you everything to live healthy and perfect. You can be healthy and perfect when you realize that you already are. You might wonder that if you are already perfectly healthy, then what's the purpose of this book? The purpose of this book is so you can realize that you are already perfectly created. Now, if you are sick that's because you have one or more of the four bodies imbalanced. For example: You may go to the gym, or train home, eat healthy but if you are conflicted in your mind, then what does exercise and good food going to do for you?

Do not forget that you are a spirit first, then you become a physical body. Your spirit (one of the unlimited fragmentations of God) can only experience emotions through physicality. So, if you are not mentally healthy, then definitely you cannot be spiritually healthy. Your brain sends signals for all your emotions. Unhealthy mind will create unhealthy emotions/feelings. Let's put it this way: You have a few ingredients to make a cake or any food for that matter.

The ingredients (natural ones, and not unhealthy) themselves are already perfect, but how you mix them will determine the outcome of what you are creating. A wrong ingredient, or too much of one ingredient or too less of another destroys the whole thing. It is the same with you. You may eat super healthy, but the negative thoughts in your mind are the wrong ingredients which in turn will jeopardize the whole system, your way of thinking, feeling, your blood pressure, your energetic levels etc.

Many negative thoughts are bad, but also many good thoughts are bad if you are not capable of directing those thoughts (the good ones) for a good purpose, toward empowerment. Since we are analytical creatures, we will be carried away with our thoughts and will introduce other thoughts or twist the ones we already have. That's why it is very important to practice **observational routines** when no thoughts enter or exit our mind. Just simply observe anything and anyone without analyzing.

Analyzing will spring judgement. **WE ARE CREATORS**. We were given this power by the CREATOR. It is very important that you pay attention to anything you say or do, and every thought that you give them. You are the chef, the scientist, the chemist, the artist that decides what goes onto the canvas (your life). Self-control and calmness are two great qualities that everyone can practice when they innerstand who they truly are.

> Practice observation and LOVE wherever you are, and your life will truly progress and shine. Love exists in all things. Not just a romantic partner. Love is everywhere, it's around you at all times:

Love is when you appreciate your existence.

Love is in appreciating your family.

Love is when you don't judge.

Love is when you appreciate a flower, a tree, an animal, or a blade of grass.

Love is when you close your eyes and meet God face to face (although God is everywhere).

Love is when you are grateful for what you have.

Love is when you treat mistakes as lessons.

Love is when you seek knowledge and innerstanding.

Rise (not fall as you can only fall in hate) in love with everything that exists as everything has a purpose. Observation is the best tool to realize what loving all creation means. Eyes are the windows of the soul. Try and look into the eyes of a bird or an animal, what do you see? You see a LIVE creation. Have you noticed that no bird, insect, or animal will look at your knees or belly or feet. They all will look into your eyes.

Because that's where an eternal recognition and connection of creation happens. Creation is always present. No such a thing as past or future. You better realize this. Surrender you memories and expectations. Live in the moment. How would you know that you are living in the moment? When you don't invest more than a second into previous present (past) moments or in imagined present moments (future). You might ask me again because I know you are intelligent and want to know more: If I don't think about the past such as something that I need to remember what I did yesterday, so I know how to do it today, then how am I supposed to know if I erase my memory?

The point of being present is to not invest emotional and mental energy into the past or the future. The point is to be invested regularly with NOW, the present. If thoughts of the past come in your mind, tell them "Hi" and let them go peacefully, don't resist them. Let them flow. They will disappear when you don't focus on them. Control yourself, be a master of your emotions, be calm and heaven will peek through the blurry curtain and be more and more present for you to experience it at all times.

"Self-Control is strength. Right thought is mastery. Calmness is power" -James Allen

The breath of God is keeping you alive. Practice this affirmation:

God lives in me and through me
My body is strong and healthy.
God's LOVE protects every organ in my body.
Its (not HE or SHE) LOVE permeates every cell
of my body, I AM divinely protected and guided
until the end of this (lifetime) existence and all other existences.
SO SHALL IT BE

Observational thoughtless practicing is
CONSCIOUS MEDITATION

Chapter ELEVEN

HEALING FREQUENCIES

Sound has a profound effect on the human body and mind. Ever since we discovered music and shamanistic chanting, we have been pushing the boundaries of how the healing effects of sounds and frequencies can be measured. Certain sound frequencies are used as part of therapies in order to manipulate brain waves to promote healing of the body and mind. Sound frequencies can be used to treat several different kinds of ailments such as insomnia, depression, anxiety, and disorders of the nervous system. For hundreds of years scientists (not $cientists) have been conscious of the effect of the sounds on the human body. Even inaudible sound can influence human brain activity. Inaudible sounds always exist everywhere.

As I have mentioned in this book that we can only hear within a certain frequency range. An inaudible sound can be beneficial or detrimental to your health. If you are someone aware and conscious of the powers that be (imposed unnatural authorities), then you would think twice before you watch movies, tv shows, news (fake news) and other programs which may very well have inaudible sounds at specific harmful frequencies. If I was you, I would stay away from pop music. As pop was invented to pop off your brain with audible and inaudible sounds.

Classical music is a very healing genre. Classical music was invented for the purpose of healing and triggering awakening and raising consciousness. I bet everyone has heard about the GREAT AWAKENING. The awakening didn't just start in 2020 when the supposed pLandemic started. The awakening started when Christ Consciousness/Law of Love was anchored on Earth over 2000 years ago.

We have been in a period of darkness and yet an awakening, nonetheless. An awakening in very small steps as to climax now that is called "The Great Awakening". Classical music was a major part of raising the consciousness of people, even though it may have not seemed so, the coding/DNA light codes were unlocking in people's bodies, at a very slow rate, parallel with the level of people's consciousness at that time. Beside listening to Beethoven, and other classical musicians, do not forget to listen to **Mozart's Sonata in D K448**. It activates DNA light codes.

Your cellular make up allows for absorption of frequencies and signals that have profound and lasting effects.

What you listen to, must be chosen very carefully. The masses can be subdued by negative powerful music frequencies that are in disharmony with how humans' harmonious frequencies operates. Consumption of negative frequency such as those in Pop music is harmful much in the way that overeating is. Many artists have been encouraged (subconsciously by benevolent beings through dreams or otherwise). They are encouraged to compose music in the key of D (major).

The moon is purposely regulated so that you are devoid of the proper amount of the absorption of light/codes. The key of D at this time is aligned with the position of the Moon and the position of luminosity. It is helping you to realign with the Moon and its luminosity. How does this work? The frequency obtained from specific musical keys can change the direction of the light waves. It is an on-going global attempt to shift the light waves.

The sound waves are being produced through musical composition collectively using a key choice-"the key of D". So, by composing music in the key of D we are redirecting the light our way (Great Awakening?). Light is information, so as you are very aware there is a lot of information circulating around about everything.

How did that happen? We are creators, we manifest the light (light codes) into reality, with the help of those benevolent beings helping us from a higher realm/dimensions. It is not impossible that those other beings could be us from a more advanced timeline. Thanks to the musical key change and the rise by .5 hz change of the Schuman resonance it saved us from another physical flood.

So, be grateful to be alive as we were so close to not exist anymore in this realm, ever. For more information on the key of D subject (and a lot more information that will make you question this reality) and other real information, including Akashic Records I suggest you read the books:

Man Being-Volume 1 By Dramos and Bohemias
Man Being-Volume 2 By Dramos and Bohemias
DNA IN THE SANDS OF TIME By J.Justice

All these 3 books have information from higher realms. (**Akashic Records /** Book of LIFE or The Living LIBRARY)

Below there is a brief explanation of 10 different harmonious frequencies. Listen to these frequencies during meditation, while asleep and during the day whenever you have time (which you do, as you can't perform actions with your ears, well you can but each to their own)). Listening to these healing, empowering frequencies will amplify the experience.

Do not think and expect that miraculously your DNA will be repaired, pain removed, relationship healed etc by just listening to these frequencies while at the same time you live the same life as before where not eating healthy, having negative thoughts, not being grateful, gossiping etc. These frequencies will have to be combined with a lifestyle change. If you are in a bad relationship, don't think that you are going to only listen to the 639 hz frequency and it will all work out.

A relationship is between two physical beings that have emotions, memories, feelings, constant thinking, imagination, expectations, anxiety, fear, ungratefulness etc. So, you see, there is much more to health than just listening to music. Personally, listening to healing frequencies improved my life tenfold.

But I wasn't just listening to these kinds of frequencies. I started exercising regularly, practiced semen retention, eating much healthier, practiced solitude so I could hear the true ME that was deep buried within and many other things I did which all are in this book. You could find music/healing music online by simple research and/or download an app that converts the music that you have on your phone/computer which is tuned at the disharmonious detrimental 440 hz frequency to 432Hz or any of the others from the chart. (4+4=8, it doesn't add to 3, 6 or 9, you will see below why).

BALANCING AND HEALING FREQUENCIES

174 hz Removes pain
285 hz Influences energy field
396 hz Transforms grief into joy and guilt into forgiveness
417 hz Facilitates change, removes subconscious blockages
432 hz Miracle tone of nature
528 hz Repairs DNA, stimulates love and restores equilibrium
639 hz Heals/strengthens relationships, family
741 hz Awaken intuition, helps you return to balance
852 hz Attracts soul tribes (like minded individuals)
963 hz CONNECTS YOU WITH LIGHT AND SPIRIT

Little known interesting fact is that if each 3 digits number frequency is added until it remains a single digit, it will equal to 3, 6 or 9. The magic Universal numbers. For example: 174 hz = 1+7+4=12 1+2=3. You can try and add all of the above frequencies and you will see that they all will add to either 3, 6 or 9. As Nicolas Tesla said:

"If you only knew the magnificence of the 3,6 and 9, then you would have the key to the Universe

In gematria you add numbers until a single digit remains. Previously I mentioned the 440 hz frequency tuning. In 1953 the frequency which all musical instruments were tuned at, was changed from 432 hz (harmonious) to 440 hz (disharmonious). 432 hz is known as the beat of the earth. It has many healing benefits.

But when under the 440 hz frequency, it causes the brain to grow agitated. In WW2 (World War two) the Nazis would use this (440 hz) frequency against their enemies to easily control them and their thoughts.

Of course, if you control someone's thoughts, you control their life, their destiny. So that's why it is of great importance to listen to healing frequencies. That's why they are called healing frequencies. Good Music is food for the soul, bad one is bad right? Just like good and bad food decide the health of your physical vehicle (body).

All of us think that what we think is our thoughts, are they? Think again. Undo the damage so you can have healthy coherent balanced thoughts, and emotions.

"Music is a form of **ART**

That goes in the ears straight to the **HEART**

Opening yourself to it EVERY **DAY**

You have no choice but to always be **OKAY**

IS MAGIC REAL?

There is no such a thing as MAGIC in the sense that something can be experiences only by specific (rare) people. Magic is considered rare and amazing because of lack of knowledge and innerstanding. Depending on the level of acceptance many things that are considered regular/normal to some, can be considered a MAGIC to others. Fasting is **MAGIC**.

Your body heals itself through fasting. People indulge in food by eating mindlessly. If they knew the power of the Magic pills (seen and unseen) such as:

Diaphragmatic breathing
Fasting,
Raw food diet,
Meditation,
Semen Retention,
Urine Therapy,
Solitude,
Conscious Observation,
Opening The Heart (loving unconditionally),

then we would be living a collectively PARADISE LIFE. Between Hell and Heaven, it is you. In the center of the scale. Would you lean toward distraction or toward Rebuilding Heaven on Earth and Pave the golden path for the next generations with empowerment, unconditional love, gratefulness, gratitude, will and determination? Only your belief dictates if it is possible or not.

All these Magic Pills are produced by you. No need to use any external fake pill. All that is needed to uncover the hidden **Heaven** within, is your awareness, will and determination to improve and progress continuously.

You are THE Alchemist.
You are THE MAGIC.

Your belief of something being possible or not possible dictates the *SUCCESS* or *FAILURE* that you can achieve.

What are you waiting for?
Explore your powers. Be aware of your qualities/talents and apply them

consciously so that your life can improve. Believe enough to manifest what you deserve.

"AS YOU BELIEVE, SO SHALL IT BE"

*****

◆ ◆ ◆

If you enjoyed or absorbed/learned anything of value, please take a few moments and give a review on **Amazon**.

Thank you

◆ ◆ ◆

ACKNOWLEDGEMENT

I am grateful to everyone that have motivated me in progressing in life. Some of those people have inspired me to write my previous book and this one. There are too many to mention them all. In no particular order:

Bartlomiej Wójcicki
Joseph Szyszka
Jodie Gien
Tuyen,
@Mikefperry,
Cosmic Kelsey
Natalie S. Haller
J.J
Ilirjan K.

If I forgot to mention your (whoever you may be) name, just know that you are not your name. You are a multidimensional heavenly being. Identifying with your name (being attached to that illusion), you limit yourself.

Thank you

ABOUT THE AUTHOR

Saimir Kercanaj

Saimir is a passionate writer and an artist. After many years working for corporations, decided to pursue what makes him happy, which is art/creating. Saimir is on a mission to spread knowledge and innerstanding about life. He feels he must share his gifts with the world because he truly believes that we all are ONE and deserve to be happy and united. Working for many corporations, having dealt with thousands of people during his lifetime and with his inner knowing, gave him tremendous insight about the world and everything in it. He will continue spreading truth in hopes that all humanity will unite and becomes ONE.

I Am The Key That Opens All Doors

An easy Philosophical/Spiritual approach to daily life.
" Life is your companion, death is your friend. When you embrace them both, there is no beginning and there is no end".- SAIMIR KERCANAJ

We all are energy dressed up in matter.
Since the beginning of falling from grace, we humans have always been wondering about our purpose in life. The answer has always been so simple and yet so difficult for us to innerstand. In this book you will be shown that the answer is so easy. It's within your grasp. Life is not difficult, we humans make it so.
To see the Light, you must first go blind.
Lose all the layers of indoctrinations that have been piling up all your life so you can actually see for the first time. That's the moment when you are truly born. You may be 25, 50 or 70, but if you haven't first fought the darkness within, then you aren't born yet. Physical and metaphysical are two sides of the same coin. You need to innerstand and practice them both to see the bigger picture.

"I AM THE KEY THAT OPENS ALL DOORS" points out a creative and positive way to turn on your inner Light, so you can shine and see clear and get out of the darkness that you have been put to, from a lifetime of conditioning from outside noises that have muffled up your own inner voice.
Unleash the power that resides deep within the center of the sacred place, deep within your heart. Question your existence. Question everything. The answer to a question must always lead

to another question.

Discover the power of being YOU. Discover your "I AM". Find out the key to happiness that exists within you. Find the KEY THAT OPENS ALL DOORS. "I AM" takes you on a journey so you can recognize both physical and metaphysical aspects of you.

Within this book you will also have the pleasure to enjoy and admire over 25 hand drawn artworks from the author of this book.

Attention: ONLY the paperback version of the book has over 25 artworks

Self Empowerment: Book 1

SELF empowering guide.

An easy to read and innerstand (understand) content. Depending on the level that you may be, some things you may understand them right away and some others you will understand them at a later time when your consciousness has expanded even more. Words are the same for everyone but can be innerstood (understood) differently by anyone. Whether it's poetry or quotes (an elaboration of them), it's about empowerment. To trigger inner knowing in you, so you don't stay stuck in destructive thinking patterns.

The poetry is also designed to empower you and not bury you deeper by reminding you of darkness without giving you a solution.

_____

ENJOY WHAT YOU HAVE

Be happy with what you have
or be destroyed from what you need
the choice is always yours
to choose gratitude or greed

Nothing belongs to you

not even yourself
you don't need possessions
you need help

help exists within yourself
you are your own savior
get your mind off of possessions
they are not real, they are delusions

you owe nothing, not even your soul
don't delude yourself, empty your mind
admire the creation, admire everything
be one with the world, be one with the king

the king of all that is, the king of all that will be
the king that gave you "life", so you can be free
the king is the Creator, the Supreme Divine
you have been chosen; can't you see the S I G N?

All the content of this book is about empowering you to be a better person than you were yesterday.

Limitless Potential

Limitless potential
Is a book that explores and gives solution to manifest the life that you want. All the potential that exists within yourself, is waiting to be unleashed. You and only you possess the key to your lock.

Journey to self realization
is a thorough explanation of what is holding you back in the three-dimensional distorted reality, and how to leave behind the weight so you can fly straight to 5D peace, love and bliss reality. It is an easy path when you realize that you are the captain to

your ship. You decide to sail toward destructive rocks or toward blissful horizons.

Are you strong enough to think, speak, and behave in way that you self-empower yourself every step of the way?
Yes, you are. It is only a matter of stilling your mind, opening your heart and right there in that sacred space, the limitless potential is waiting for you to embrace and give it wings.

Dive in the vastness of your potentiality.

Become Free Through Insightful Poetry

A collection of poetry and prose.

Other books by this author

From the author of
LIMITLESS POTENTIAL: Journey to self-realization

BECOME
F R E E
Through
INSIGHTFUL
POETRY

poetry and prose

Saimir Kercanaj

SAIMIR KERCANAJ
I AM
THE KEY
THAT OPENS ALL DOORS

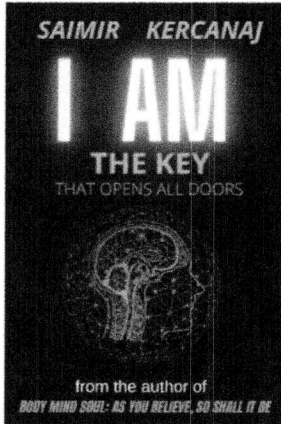

from the author of
BODY MIND SOUL: AS YOU BELIEVE, SO SHALL IT BE

from the author of
BODY MIND SOUL & I AM THE KEY THAT OPENS ALL DOORS

SELF
EMPOWERMENT

Book 1

SAIMIR
K E R C A N A J
poetry, quotes, deep thoughts

Saimir X. Kercanaj
you are not a
STRAWMAN

YOU ARE THE
ZYGOTE

"All present and accounted for"
from fertilization to last breath:

KNOW THAT YOU DON'T KNOW

GAIN
WISDOM
THROUGH PRACTICED
KNOWLEDGE

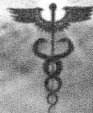

RIMIAS K. NEO

From the author of
SELF EMPOWERMENT - BOOK 1

Limitless
POTENTIAL
Journey To Self-Realization

A guide
to discovering your potential

Saimir Kercanaj

RECOMMENDED READING

You Are The One...Pine G. Land
Rebuild Yourself From Within by J.J. and TAMO
Superpower Breathing... Patricia Bragg
I AM the key that opens all doors.................... Saimir Kercanaj
The Tao of health sex and longevity................... Daniel P. Reid
You Are The Remedy...Anna Replica
How men turn evil - Humanity's dark side........ Jordan Preston
The detox miracle sourcebook............................ Robert Morse
DNA in the sands of time.. J. Justice
The pineal eye.. Dr. M. Doreal
Man Being – Go to the Light Volume II... Dramos & Bohemias

www.yogiapproved.com
www.openfit.com
www.theserpentsway.com
www.mindmasternews.com
www.yogabykarina.com
www.fitsri.com

GLOSSARY

Telomeres - Either of the sections of DNA occurring at the ends of a chromosome. Telomeres are made of repetitive sequences of non-coding DNA that protect the chromosome from damage. Each time a cell divides, the telomeres become shorter. Eventually the telomeres become so short that the cell no longer divides. It becomes short over time from eating, thinking, and behaving unhealthy. There is no reason why we should age when we live our life as intended in alignment with nature. Eating, feeling, thinking healthy will elongate the telomeres/DNA, and you wouldn't age.

Meridians - Are energetic highways in the human body. Meridians allow for the flow of energy, known as "Qi," pronounced Chee, to circulate throughout the body. Meridians exist in corresponding pairs and each meridian has multiple acupuncture points along the pathways. An example is the bottom of the feet where massaging specific areas of the bottom of the feet, is like massaging the heart, liver, pancreas etc.

Peristalsis - Is a wavelike muscular contraction of the digestive tract or other tubular structures by which contents (feces) are forced/propelled onward toward the opening (or exit).

Chakras - Are spiritual energetic points in the human body described in yogic philosophy as centers of vital energy. There are seven chakras in the human body. There are more but there are only seven in the physical body. You can reach enlightenment when all 7 chakras are opened and aligned with each other. I'm thinking of writing a small book based on the chakras. Maybe that will be the next one.

Kundalini - Is energy that lies dormant at the base of the spine until it is activated by practicing yoga/meditation. After this energy is awakened it channels upward through all seven chakras in a spiral (serpent) motion, in the process of spiritual perfection. This serpent/energy will not awaken until you have a healthy balance between physical/emotional/mental and spiritual bodies.

Soul - It is your immaterial self, the unseen you. It is your true immortal self-separable from the physical body at death. Your soul gives life to your physical body. Any harm you do to your body, you also do to your immaterial one.

Chee - The human body (physical or metaphysical) is a force of energy, and that energy (Chee) is everywhere. Which means that you are part of everything. Everything is connected to you and vice versa. In Asian healing, they practice the balance of Chee, your energy. Which the Western medicine is far behind. Balancing your qi/Chee, you receive maximum health and wellness benefits. Of course, it has to be combined with healthy eating and healthy thinking. You cannot get your energy balanced by consuming processed poison, alcohol, meat etc. Technically, the above things I mentioned consume you and not the other way around.

Yin/Yang - Is a concept of dualism in ancient Asian philosophy. We have dark-light, negative-positive, good-bad, love-hate, rich-poor etc. These are some examples of yin and yang. This concept of dualism describes how obviously opposite or contrary forces may actually be complimentary, interconnected, and interdependent in the natural world, and how they may give rise to each other as they interrelate to one another. In Chinese cosmology, the universe creates itself out of a primary chaos of material energy, organized into the cycles of Yin and Yang and formed into objects (land, trees, oceans, plants etc) and lives (humans, animals, birds, bugs etc). Yin is the receptive and Yang is the active principle, seen in all forms of change and difference such as the annual cycle (winter/summer), the landscape (north-facing shade and south-facing brightness), sexual coupling (female/male), the formation of both men and women as characters and socio-political history (order and disorder).

Nephilim - Nephilim are a race of beings or people that are giants and very strong compared to us. They are believed to be the fallen angels (mentioned in sacred, ancient texts) that created us the homosapiens.

Homeostasis - Homeostasis is a state of equilibrium, as in an organism or cell, maintained by self-regulating processes. It is the state of steady internal chemical and physical conditions maintained by living systems. The body maintains homeostasis by controlling a host of variables ranging from body temperatures, blood PH, blood glucose levels to fluid balance, sodium, potassium, and calcium ion concentrations. It is crucial that you take care of your body, meaning to keep your body in the homeostasis state where the body can fix itself automatically when foreign opportunistic organisms enter your body. If your body is flooded with bad food, bad water (or not enough water), bad thoughts, fear, anxiety etc, then your body will not be able to regulate itself as it will already be choked by poison.

Mystery School -"The term Mystery School Comes directly from Ancient Egypt and refers not to a specific time or place in Ancient Egypt, but rather timeless secret teachings, passed down through word of mouth, through priests and priestesses, initiates and royalty, and encrypted into the temple themselves, concealed and enshrined behind a veil of hieroglyph and symbolism." -John Anthony West

What is not directly visible in the material world around us, the mind can intuitively see-through symbols. Now, you can guess how your subconsciousness can be programmed through symbols, hieroglyphs when watching movies, Tv shows, on the internet, or when there are symbols written on magazines or textbooks etc. There is no such thing as bad information. The problem is when the information is hijacked and used for nefarious purposes.

Sanskrit - Sanskrit is a classical language of South Asia belonging to the Indo-Aryan branch of the Indo-European languages. Sanskrit is the sacred language of Hinduism, the language of classical Hindu philosophy and of historical texts of Buddhism and Jainism.

Printed in Great Britain
by Amazon